Why do Tampa Bay fans die young?
They want to.

The seat beside Jim at the Redskins
playoff game was empty, so Jim said
to the man on the other side, "Pretty
incredible to have a no-show at a
game like this."
The man said, "That's my wife's seat."
"I see," said Jim. "She sick?"
"No. She's dead."
"Oh," said Jim. "Couldn't you find a
friend or relative to come with you?"
"Nope," said the man. "They're all at
her funeral."

To err is human. To blame it on
someone else is doubles.

1,001 GREAT SPORTS JOKES

JEFF ROVIN

A SIGNET BOOK

SIGNET
Published by the Penguin Group
Penguin Books USA Inc., 375 Hudson Street,
New York, New York 10014, U.S.A.
Penguin Books Ltd, 27 Wrights Lane,
London W8 5TZ, England
Penguin Books Australia Ltd, Ringwood,
Victoria, Australia
Penguin Books Canada Ltd, 2801 John Street,
Markham, Ontario, Canada L3R 1B4
Penguin Books (N.Z.) Ltd, 182-190 Wairau Road,
Auckland 10, New Zealand

Penguin Books Ltd, Registered Offices:
Harmondsworth, Middlesex, England

First published by Signet, an imprint of New American Library, a division of Penguin Books USA Inc.

First Printing, May, 1991
10 9 8 7 6 5 4 3 2 1

REGISTERED TRADEMARK—MARCA REGISTRADA

PRINTED IN THE UNITED STATES OF AMERICA

BOOKS ARE AVAILABLE AT QUANTITY DISCOUNTS WHEN USED TO PROMOTE PRODUCTS OR SERVICES. FOR INFORMATION PLEASE WRITE TO PREMIUM MARKETING DIVISION, PENGUIN BOOKS USA INC., 375 HUDSON STREET, NEW YORK, NEW YORK 10014.

INTRODUCTION

(Sung to the tune of
"Take Me Out to the Ball Game")

If you like jokes 'bout football,
If you like 'em 'bout golf.
Here is a book that is just for you—
All kinds of sports jokes and sports riddles too!
These are jokes intended for grown-ups
(Plus some you can tell the kids!)
So don't wait—there's laughter in store
At the old ball game!

NOTE

Like most joke books, we've picked on a few minorities herein (especially the Poles, a group to which the author belongs). Please don't be offended. As the croquet failure said regarding his game, "This I do with mallets toward none. . . ."

BASEBALL

Q: What do the major league slugger and a baker
   have in common?
A: They both know it takes a great batter to
   make great dough.

Q: Why are most managers like diapers?
A: They're always on somebody's butt, and
   they're usually full of crap.

When room service arrived with the major
league star's breakfast, the waiter saw a dress,
blouse, and female undergarments scattered
around the room.

"Would you like me to bring anything for your
wife?" the waiter inquired.

The player's brow furrowed, and he handed
the waiter a five-dollar bill. "Good idea. Bring
me some postcards from the newsstand."

Q: From what did the pitcher and his pregnant
   wife both suffer?
A: Complete exhaustion in the ninth.

Q: Why is playing baseball like dating a Jewish American Princess?

A: You won't get to first base without a diamond.

Catcher Carter Gary never saw it coming.

The pitch was way outside, and as he dived to get it, the batter surprised him by swinging; the bat connected hard with the back of Gary's catching hand, shattering every bone and tendon.

Gary passed out, and the next thing he knew he was lying in a hospital bed looking up at the team physician.

"God, w-what happened?" Gary asked.

"Well, there's good news and there's bad news."

Swallowing hard, Gary said, "Gimme the bad news first, doc."

"The bad news is that you'll never play again. Your hand was destroyed and we had to amputate it."

"Lord, no!" wailed Gary. "What *good news* could there possibly be?"

"The guy who replaced you wants to buy your glove."

Then there was the philandering baseball player who cheated on his wife so often he was finally thrown out at home.

Q: Why aren't there any leper pitchers?
A: They're always throwing their arm out.

Milt Famie was the greatest pitcher ever to take the mound for the Baltimore team. His only failing was that he couldn't hold his liquor, so the coaches and his teammates made sure he never got near a drink before a game.

However, the Mets team was smarter, and the night before the last game of the World Series, several players lured Milt Famie from his hotel room by pretending to be Hollywood producers interested in making a movie of Milt's life.

They fed him beer after beer, and the next day Milt threw nothing but balls. The Mets won big, and during the postgame press conference, the New York manager was asked about the victory.

Not wanting to take anything away from the rest of the sterling Baltimore team, the manager said succinctly, "My friend, it's the beer that made Milt Famie walk us."

The batter had incredible power, but he was the dumbest creature on two legs, unable to tell a strike from a ball. During practice one day, the batting coach came up with what he thought was an ideal solution and called the slugger to the dugout.

"Listen," said the coach. "I'm going to tell the second baseman to keep an eye on the ball. When he shakes his head, you don't swing. When he nods, you do swing. Got it?"

The batter furrowed his brow. "I see 'im shakes his head *no*, 'at means I don't swing. He *nods*, 'at means I swing."

The coach nodded.

His head soared gracefully into right field.

The major league manager was startled when a turkey wandered into spring training one day.

"I'd like to play for your team," the turkey said.

Convinced that this was some kind of gag, the manager decided to go along with it. "Sure," he said. "Get out there and show me what you can do."

The turkey grabbed a glove and scurried out to center field. The first batter hit a grounder, and much to the manager's surprise, the plucky bird scooped it up and burned it over to first. A line drive was caught inches above the ground. A certain home run was prevented when the bird fluttered up and grabbed the ball as it soared over the fence.

After the inning was over, the manager ran over to the turkey.

"You were brilliant!" he declared. "I want to sign you at once!"

"Under one condition," replied the bird.

"Anything!"

"We play through November."

Q: What did the clever manager do to prevent the opposing team from stealing bases?
A: He fired his batboy and hired Batman.

Q: What position is "light field"?
A: It's opposite "left field" on the Tokyo Giants.

Two anthropologists were lost in the jungles of New Guinea when they stumbled upon a cannibal village. Fortunately, the natives were well provisioned and didn't eat them. Indeed, the cannibals invited the anthropologists to do some shopping in their local food store.

Not wishing to insult their hosts, the anthropologists entered the hut and looked at the prices.

"Fifty z'boolies for a pound of human intestines," said one of the visitors as she read off the prices, "fifty-five for a pound of liver . . . and six *hundred* z'boolies for a pound of baseball manager's heart! My goodness, it must be delicious!"

"It has nothing to do with delicious," said the shopkeeper. "Do you know how many baseball managers we have to kill to get a pound of heart?"

Not that baseball managers have it easy. One had to get out of baseball because of illness and exhaustion: the owner was sick and tired of losing.

Q: What's the difference between an owner and a pit bull?
A: A jacket and tie.

Q: Why are owners such good laxatives?
A: They annoy the crap out of everyone.

Sad, but true: the romantic escapades of a playboy pitcher ended suddenly when he caught a line drive on the fly.

Mark ran up to his friend at school. "Did you hear about the tiger with *three balls*?"
"No."
"He got a fourth and walked."

Then there was the guy who didn't know a thing about baseball and got irate when he heard that a pitcher who was earning two million a year needed relief.

Remember that ace fielder, the turkey? Well, it seems the same team had another strange encounter with the animal kingdom when a horse sauntered over to the bullpen one day during practice.

"Gimme a shot," he said to the manager. "I can hit like no one you've ever seen."

"A talking horse that can hit," said the manager. "This I've gotta see."

The horse selected a bat, stepped up to the plate, and waited for the pitch. It was a screaming fastball, but the horse was undaunted. There was a crack that shattered the sound barrier, and the ball literally smoked as it rocketed over the fence. Sneering, the pitcher hurled a screwball. The horse bunted, and the ball bobbed and weaved as three different players tried to catch it. Flustered, the pitcher tossed a picture-perfect curveball. The horse drove it straight down the third-base line.

The manager ran out to home plate, contract in hand, and immediately signed the horse.

The next day, the horse was assigned the cleanup spot on the roster. It was first inning, bases loaded, when the stallion stepped up to the plate.

The opposing pitcher snickered and threw a sinker, his expression sobering when the ball rose like a Roman candle and sailed out over the parking lot.

The bullpen cheered, but the animal just stood there.

"Hey, horse!" the manager screamed. "Ya gotta *run!*"

The horse turned. "Jerk! If I could run, I'd still be at Belmont!"

As the ball flew off the sandlot diamond, one kid in the outfield yelled, "Jeepers! It's a run home!"

The batter yelled, "You mean, a home run!"

"No, a run home! You smashed somebody's windshield!"

Q: Why does a pitcher raise one leg when he winds up?

A: Because if he raised them both, he'd fall down.

The elementary-school teacher gave her students an assignment to make a list of the ten greatest Americans. After an hour, she asked for the papers to be passed up. Little Keith stopped tapping his chin with the pencil and began writing furiously.

"Time's up," the teacher said.

"Sorry," Keith said, running up with the paper, "but I finally just decided on the manager and shortstop."

Q: Why did the preschooler love baseball cards?

A: Even though he couldn't read the stats, he could look at the pitchers.

The pitcher wasn't having a good day. Finally, the manager came out to the mound.

"Sorry," he said, "but I'm sending you to the showers."

"You can't," said the pitcher. "I'm hitting my stride. Besides, look who's on deck. I struck him out twice and walked him once."

"I know," said the manager, "but it's still the same inning."

Moose came to the office with a big bruise on his forehead.

"What happened to you?" a co-worker asked.

"I went camping with my friend Clyde, the baseball player."

"And he hit you?"

"No," said Moose. "I asked him to pitch the tent, and that's just what he did."

Q: What do you call a manager who'd sell his soul for a slugger like the Babe?

A: Ruthless.

One little leaguer said to the other, "Hey, wanna see something swell?"

"Sure!" said the other, and the first kid hit him in the eye with the bat.

Mr. Tibbs walked into the bar with his dog C.B.

"You'll have to leave," the bartender said. "Dogs aren't allowed in here."

"But this isn't an ordinary dog," said Tibbs. "He talks."

"Does he?" said the bartender. "Fine. You make him talk, I'll let him stay."

Mr. Tibbs looked at the dog. "C.B.—what do you find on top of a house?"

"Roof!" barked the dog.

"What kind of collar did Sir Walter Raleigh wear?"

"Ruff!" answered the dog.

The bartender frowned. "Who're you trying to con? He's just *barking*! Any dog could do that."

"You're wrong, and I'll prove it," said Mr. Tibbs. "C.B., who was the greatest Yankee player in history?"

"Ruth!" yipped the dog.

"Mister, you're an ass—" snapped the bartender.

With a scowl, the dog turned to the bartender and said, "Who, then? DiMaggio?"

The St. Louis Cardinals decided to give away birds during a game and sent their promotional director out to buy them.

The young man walked into a pet store. "I'd like bird seed," he told the owner.

"Certainly. For what kind of bird?"

"Cardinals," he said. "I want enough to grow two hundred of them."

A baseball player is someone who, if he isn't fired with enthusiasm, is fired with enthusiasm.

Ms. Ackerman faced the elementary-school geography class and said, "Can anyone tell me where Chicago is?"

Little Billy rose and said, "They're playing in Pittsburgh today."

The baseball star had quite a day: married in the morning, then off to play ball in the afternoon. With the game tied in the ninth inning, the player was afraid the game would go into extra innings and his new wife would be upset. Thus, as soon as he got the chance, he stole home, sliding on his belly the last few yards. He scored, but the price was high: he scraped his genitals raw.

The team physician bandaged his chafed member, and the sullen player made his way home.

That night, the woman undid her robe and came to him.

"Here, my darling," she said. "No man has ever touched me before."

Trying to put the best face on things, the player disrobed and said, "Here, hon. Mine's still in the original wrapper."

So many players had caught herpes on the road, they finally organized a pair of support groups: the National and American Lesions.

Q: How many Yankee managers does it take to screw in a light bulb?
A: Four. No one's ever around long enough to do the job himself.

The pope and the umpire arrived at the Pearly Gates at the same time. After welcoming them, Saint Peter walked them to their respective abodes.

The umpire was shown to his heavenly home first, a stunning mansion with marble columns and multitiered fountains inside and out. After Saint Peter wished the umpire well, he led the pope to his home, which was little more than a shack, with rotted walls and a leaking roof.

"I don't understand," said the pope. "Why did the umpire get such a beautiful home while I'm given this hovel?"

"Well," said Saint Peter, "the truth is, we've got dozens of popes up here, but very few umpires."

Then there was the disappointed Pirates fan who noted that the Allegheny goes right by Three Rivers Stadium, and she didn't blame it!

Q: Speaking of the Allegheny, why aren't Pittsburgh fans allowed to swim in it?
A: They leave a ring.

Q: How are major league pitchers like a tin of Crisco?
A: Both have lard in the can.

The young girl's mother screamed, "You went out with that lady-killer Deke Tyler—the major league pitcher?"

"Gimme a break, Mom. He's a dream."

The older woman shook her head. "I hope you went into it with your eyes wide open."

"Sure did," said the girl. "And don't men look silly when they come?"

The elderly woman approached the catcher at a baseball-card autographing session.

"And what position do you play?" she asked.

The catcher replied, "Sort of crouched down, with my hands chest-high."

Q: How many Yankees fans does it take to change a light bulb?

A: Two. One to change it, and one to go on and on about how good the old bulb was, and the one before that, and . . .

One young baseball fan said to his friend, "When I grow up, I'm gonna play ball for the Orioles."

The other boy thumped his chest. "Me?" he said. "When I grow up, they're gonna have to pay me in money, not birds."

It was a Tuesday afternoon during spring training, and the man turned to the little boy sitting next to him in the grandstand.

"It's none of my business," said the man, "but shouldn't you be in school?"

"Nah," said the kid, "it's cool. I've got the German measles."

Rufus came home with a brand-new baseball.

"Where'd you get that?" his mother asked.

"Mickey gave it to me for doing him a favor."

"How nice!" his mother said, beaming. "What favor was that?"

Rufus replied, "I stopped hitting him with my bat."

Q: Which league plays baseball with coal instead of with a hardball?
A: The miner league.

"Baseball!" snapped Irv's wife. "Why don't you ever dream of me instead of baseball?"

Irv gasped, "And miss my turn at bat?

Q: What's the difference between a pickpocket and an umpire?
A: One steals watches. . . .

Then there was the slugger who refused to join the union when he learned they might be called out on strikes . . .

. . . and the clergyman who gently corrected a boy who thought that Adam was a baseball player, because he fell from grace, "In the big inning. . . ."

Young Victor said to his older brother Chris, "Did you know that it takes longer to run from second to third than from third to home?"

Chris scratched his head. "How can that be?"

"There's a short stop between them."

Q: What's the difference between a can of Raid and a terrible outfielder?

A: One drops flies, and the other also misses grounders.

Q: Who's the most admired man in baseball history?

A: Francis Scott Key. He knew all the words to "The Star-Spangled Banner."

Then there's the fan who pointed out that an umpire is an expert on baseball in the same way that a hooker is an expert on love.

The brawny catcher stood before the judge.

"Mr. DiFate," said the judge, "you're charged with chasing the umpire to the top tier and throwing him off."

"I'm genuinely sorry," said DiFate. "I did it in a fit of anger."

"I appreciate that," the judge replied, "but don't you realize how dangerous that might have been to someone walking in the parking lot?"

The rookie was undressing after a night game when he happened to glance over at Clyde, a black player.

"Man," he said, "it's true what they say about you guys! You're really hung."

Clyde said, "Nah, it isn't just blacks. You've got to know how to do the exercise."

"What exercise?"

"Before you go to bed each night, just slap your John Thomas three times."

Willing to try, the rookie went home. His wife was already asleep, and pausing beside the bed, he did as he'd been instructed and slapped his member three times.

His wife stirred. "Clyde . . . is that you?"

As Isaac lay in the hospital, awaiting a heart for transplanting, his surgeon came running into the room.

"Good news!" he said. "We've got two hearts

available—a priest's heart for $50,000 or a baseball team owner's heart for $1 million."

"Wh-why are the prices so different?" Isaac asked weakly.

The doctor replied, "One of them has never been used."

Q: What do you call a Cleveland player who refused to sign his contract?
A: A wouldn't Indian.

The pitcher reported for spring training and drew angry stares from the manager: he'd put on at least twenty pounds, all of it around the waist.

"My *God*," the manager screamed, "you been living on Twinkies all winter? You're going on a diet *now*, you tub o' lard. I swear, if that gut was on a woman, I'd think she was pregnant."

Trying to regain some of his battered dignity, the pitcher replied, "It was. She is."

Q: Why did the Irishmen bring a TV to the stadium?
A: So they could see what was happening at their favorite bar.

Then there was the Giants star who bought his wife a wig while he was on the road, after learning that she was getting balled in his absence . . .

... and the dense Pittsburgh player who was asked by a fan if he'd gone to New York by bus or plane, and answered, "I don't know. The front office made the reservations."

Q: What's the difference between a Topps collector and a team playing against St. Louis?
A: One saves cards, the other likes throwing them out.

Q: How can you tell a well-mannered ballplayer?
A: He doesn't blow on his soup in a restaurant, he fans it with his cap.

Q: What do you get when you cross a Yankees slugger and a renowned geneticist?
A: Mickey Mendel.

Q: What did the Cubs fanatic demand when he went to the dentist?
A: Baseball caps.

Q: What's the real value of old-timers day?
A: It gives the fans a chance to let off esteem.

Q: What do you call a kid who's too young to play in the little league?
A: A peanut bunter.

Then there was the L.A. player with an aptitude for drawing. Friends called him the artful Dodger.

More amazing by far, however, was the bird who learned to bat and was signed by the mynah leagues.

Q: Who sings "The Star-Spangled Banner" at Shea Stadium?
A: A Mets soprano.

How could you give an *F* to little Huey, a baseball fan who seldom thought of anything else? When his geography teacher asked him to tell the class something about Toronto, he rose, cleared his throat, and said, "When you hit the ball, you have Toronto first base."

Q: What do you call someone who imitates the batting style of one of the Detroit Tigers?
A: A copycat.

After a hard game, the unthinkably rude umpire went home and settled into his easy chair. His young son came over to sit on his lap and was promptly shooed off.

"My boy," said the man, "the son never sits on the brutish umpire."

Then there was the lecherous first baseman who molested a lady fan and was debased....

Q: What's the best way to describe the Yankees when Mickey retired?
A: They were dismantled.

Q: What's the difference between a catcher who's sent to the hospital and the catcher who replaces him?
A: One is admitted, the other's a mitt added.

Q: What says, "First, second, third, home, first, second, third, home . . . ?"
A: A Polish slugger walking up to the plate.

Q: What's the difference between a batter who bunts badly and England's Charles II?
A: One is thrown out at first, the other was throne out, at first.

"Ah, yes," said the retired New York ballplayer to his nephew, "I remember the year the Mets won their first World Series."

"What did you play?" asked the boy.

"I was left—"

"Wow! Left field!"

"No," said the man sadly. "Left out."

Q: How can you tell that Tahitians are smarter than Americans?

A: When it came to picking a national pastime, they chose sex.

Q: What do you call an insomniac umpire?

A: A prick that stays up all night.

Q: What do Michael Jackson and the Braves have in common?

A: They both wear gloves, though no one understands why.

Q: What's the difference between a typical Mariners score and a game spent in the highest row in the Kingdome?

A: One's zero in nine innings, the other's nine innings in row Z.

Q: Who takes care of the Orioles when they're ill?
A: The Baltimore MD.

It came to pass that immortal pitcher Cy Young got bopped in the left eye with a line drive. He was told to wear a patch, but refused, saying it would hurt his depth perception.

Still, before he went to the mound, his coach warned him to rely mostly on his sighted orb: "Remember," said he, "only the good eye, Young."

Roger and Casey were walking through a graveyard.

"Hey, look at this," Roger said, pointing to a headstone. "It says, 'Here lies an umpire and a good man.'"

"So," said Casey, "they're buryin' people two in a plot now."

Sign that went up on the Los Angeles high-school bulletin board in April: ANY STUDENT WHO NEEDS TO ATTEND THE FUNERAL OF A RELATIVE SHOULD NOTIFY HIS OR HER GUIDANCE COUNSELOR THE DAY OF THE GAME.

Q: What's the difference between a hardball and a dance that degenerates into an orgy?
A: None. They're both baseballs.

The contractor went to see the stadium manager in his office atop the huge arena. He opened the blueprints on the manager's desk.

"I just wanted to check a few things," he said. "We've got the bottom tier being done in red."

"Right," said the manager.

Excusing himself, he walked to a window, opened it, and shouted out, "Green on top!" Then he walked back to the desk. "Next, you want the second tier done in blue."

"Correct."

The contractor excused himself again, went to the window, yelled, "Green on top!" then returned to the desk. "After that," he said, "we've got the yellow tier."

"Yes," said the manager.

The contractor nodded, then excused himself again. This time the manager grabbed his arm. "Why is it that each time I agree to a color, you go to the window and yell, 'Green on top'?"

"Sorry," he said, "but I've got a team of Poles out there putting down your Astroturf."

Then there was the Chicago baseball star who kept three mistresses in Philadelphia and went to see them whenever he was in town. All three lived comfortably, but two of them had it really soft.

Q: What's the difference between the Padres and a man in a singles bar?
A: The man in the singles bar scores every now and then.

Trying to encourage his baseball-crazy son to be more responsible, Mr. Rogers said, "When Babe Ruth was your age, he was standing on windy street corners, selling newspapers for a penny each."

Unimpressed, the son replied, "And when he was your age, he was rich and famous."

Q: What's the difference between a player who walks and one who slides headfirst?
A: None. They're both bases on balls.

Q: How is an elusive spy like a ballplayer without a contract?
A: Both are free agents.

Q: What's the difference between baseball and dating?
A: On a date, the man still does all the pitching ... but it's the woman who has the best curves.

After his player was called out at first, the manager calmly walked out to the umpire.

"I know you like to get eight hours of sleep a day," said the manager, "but what do you do when you go home?"

Q: What's the difference between a slugger and a guy who can't get the big hit?

A: One chokes up on the bat, the other on the plate.

Q: What's the difference between Attila's arrival in Italy and a player rounding third base?

A: One's a hun in Rome ...

BASKETBALL

Q: How does a basketball coach know when his team is in first place?

A: When the spectators wave, they use more than one finger.

Timid, dumb David went to the box office at Madison Square Garden and bought a ticket to a Knicks game. He came back a few minutes later and bought another.

The clerk looked at him strangely. "Why are you here again?"

"I had no choice," he said, and glanced over his shoulder. "That man at the gate tore the last one in half."

Q: What's the difference between a revival meeting and a college basketball game?

A: At one they yell, "Stand up for Jesus," and at the other they shout, "Sit down, for Christ's sake!"

Little Wally and his father went to the high-school basketball game.

"Look at those guys move," the man said. "You wouldn't think people could have such grace *and* strength."

"But they're not people," Wally said. "They're robots."

The boy's father smiled. "Whatever makes you say that, son?"

"Because the other day, I heard sis telling her friend she went to the locker room after a game and screwed their asses off."

The truth is, Wally's sister had quite a thing for basketball players. Even though her father grounded her, she found a way to sneak out and date the only guy on the team she'd never been with.

Wilson was a six-six center, and when they were alone in the car, she quickly made her move on the Adonis-like athlete.

Much to her surprise, his endowment was far less than she'd imagined. Unable to contain her disappointment, she froze.

" 'S matter, baby?" Wilson asked.

The distraught girl blurted and pointed. "I'm sorry, but all your teammates were so ... big. Who do you expect to satisfy with that?"

Undaunted, Wilson shrugged and replied, "Me."

Q: What was the longest amateur sports competition in history?

A: The slam-dunk marathon at an all-white high school.

Olson was one of the best foul shooters in professional ball. Thus, when he started missing shot after shot in game after game, the coach took him aside.

"Listen," he said, "you've been doing squat from the foul line. Have you had your eyes checked?"

"Hell no," said the athlete. "Look for yourself—they're still brown."

Q: What's the first thing aspiring cheerleaders and aspiring players must do before they can become stars?

A: They both have to make the team.

It was the strangest thing coach Kahrs had ever seen in Olympic basketball: Every time a player pushed or traveled or hacked, the Polish referee failed to assess a penalty. Instead, he'd cup his hands to his mouth and shout out the name of a barnyard bird.

Kahrs finally had enough of this and went over to the referee.

"What do you think you're doing? Their guy elbows one of mine, you yell, 'Chicken!' They trip one of my boys, you shout, 'Hen!' What the hell's going on here?"

"What are you, stupid?" the Pole snapped. "I'm calling fowls."

Shmenge was a Polish high-school kid who excelled in basketball. Spotted by a U.S. university, he was offered a scholarship and accepted.

After a few months, he wrote home that he as playing superbly, eating well, and had grown another foot. A week later, a package arrived from his mother. In it was another sneaker.

Truth be told, Shmenge wasn't only a star hoopster, he was the greatest Polish student in history. He got his degree in just three terms: Carter's, Reagan's, and Bush's.

Why, Shmenge was so bright that the day his Polish coach brought him to the university, the athlete dazzled the Americans with his academic skills.

"How much is two plus two?" a member of the admitting board asked.

"Six," Shmenge replied.

"Not bad, eh?" the Polish coach said. "He only missed by one."

Eventually, Shmenge graduated and turned pro. Too cheap to hire an agent, he nonetheless managed to negotiate himself a $2 million contract: two bucks a year for a million years.

Q: What do you call the vehicle that takes a basketball team to the arena?
A: A blood vessel.

Q: What's the one thing a bar and a basketball court have in common?
A: Highballs left and right.

Graffiti scrawled in a New York urinal: JESUS SAVES, EWING GETS THE REBOUNDS.

Q: What do they call basketball in Honolulu?
A: Hula hoop.

Q: Why do agoraphobics make good basketball players?
A: Because they shun traveling.

And no doubt you've heard that the sportscasters who specialize in basketball have decided to form a club. The name, of course, is Full Court Press. . . .

Then there's the story of poor Rupert, the masseur for the Heat, who was fired because he rubbed the players the wrong way.

Q: What's Earl the Pearl's middle name?
A: The.

Taken away from the TV by a phone call in the last minutes of the game, Elliot asked his wife to watch and tell him who won. After all, he had a lot of money riding on the outcome.

A few minutes later, his wife walked into his study.

"What was the score?" he asked, covering the mouthpiece.

"It was 120 to 118."

"Oh, man! Who won?"

She said, "One hundred twenty did."

Then there was the basketball player who quit the team. He was getting all kinds of credit for the team's resurgence, but no cash.

Q: What do you get when you cross Jordan with a squirrel?
A: An animal that doesn't need to climb trees to stash acorns.

Q: What do you get when you cross a Port-a-Potty with Kareem Abdul-Jabbar?
A: Loo Alcindor.

Q: What do you get when you cross Dr. J with a Jackass?
A: A slam donkey.

Q: What do you call an exhibition match between two Colombian basketball stars?
A: Juan-on-Juan.

Q: What did they call the god-awful basketball team from Leningrad?
A: The no good-Knicks.

Q: What happened when the Israeli airline magnate bought the Los Angeles basketball team?
A: They changed their name to the El Al Lakers.

Q: What do they call the Detroit players after their fans have had too much to drink?
A: The pissed-ons.

Q: What nickname did they give the Boston superstar after he ate a crock of baked beans?
A: Thunderbird.

Q: What do you get when you cross a voyeur with Wilt Chamberlain?
A: A Peeping Tom that can look into second-floor windows.

A college is a place that has forty seats in the average classroom, and 10,000 seats in the average indoor arena.

A true basketball fan is one who sits in the front row and, after the game, says, "What cheerleaders?"

The Miami front office got a frantic call from their scout.

"I'm at some rinky-dink college in Arkansas," he said, "but I just saw something you wouldn't believe! Kid on the team just stood at midcourt. Every time they got him the ball, he swished a three-pointer. We've *got* to sign him!"

The general manager replied, "Schmuck, I sent you out to find me someone who was good under the boards! Sign the kid who was passing to him."

The basketball coach died and went to heaven. Immediately upon his arrival, he began assembling the greatest team this world—or the next—had ever seen.

As he was drilling his men, the phone rang; it was Satan.

"How about a little wager?" said the devil. "I've got a team that can beat yours."

"You're out of your mind!" said the coach. "Why, the greatest players in history are on my squad!"

"I know," replied Satan, "but I've got all the refs."

A big woman, her triple chins rippling, disapproved of yet another one of coach Winny Church's decisions and let him know it.

"You stink! If you were my husband, I'd feed you *poison*!"

Finally having had his fill of the woman, Church turned and said to her, "Madam, if I were your husband, I'd gladly drink it."

Then there was the sixth grader who was asked to list his three favorite sports. The basketball fanatic wrote down, "NBA basketball, college basketball, and high-school basketball."

Q: What did the referee do when the fan, a leper, gave him the finger?
A: He threw it out.

"You hear about that Polish basketball team?" one fan asked another. "They played UCLA and made every shot they took—scored over 200 points in all. But they still lost."

"Wow! UCLA must've been hitting like demons!"

"Demons, shmemons," the fan said. "No one told the Poles there was another side to the court."

Two car poolers were chatting as they drove along the Ventura Freeway.

"Y'know," said the driver, "I think the biggest mistake I ever made was going to NYU instead of UCLA."

"UCLA?" the other exclaimed. "Forget it! The only people who go there are basketball players and tramps."

The driver squeezed the wheel. "I'll have you know my wife went to UCLA."

"No kidding!" said the other. "What position did she play?"

Q: What's a Hawaiian basketball player's favorite play?
A: A lei up.

Q: How many U Conn hoopsters does it take to change a light bulb?
A: Just one, and he gets four credits for it.

It was the first time in the history of USC that the entire basketball squad showed up for a class. The class was sex education, and someone had leaked the fact that there would be an oral exam.

High-school basketball miracle Lenny Wengler was told he had to pass the simplest math quiz imaginable in order to be admitted to UCLA.

"All I want you to do is count to fifteen," the math teacher said.

Lenny looked down at his hands, began to count, got to ten, then faltered.

The teacher said, "Come on, Wengler. Can't you count *any* higher?"

Thinking hard, he raised his hands above his head and said, "One, two, three ..."

Q: Where in the library will you find Wilt Chamberlain's autobiography?
A: Under tall tales.

Then there was the sign at the gym where the college was holding open tryouts for the basketball team: IF YOU CAN PASS THROUGH THIS DOOR WITHOUT BENDING, DON'T.

Q: What kind of a baby did the center have?
A: A bouncing baby boy, of course.

Then there was the Pole who was watching TV and bet a friend twenty bucks that the center wouldn't make the foul shot. When the ball hit the rim and fell in, the Pole was distraught. Anxious to make his money back, he bet double or nothing on the instant replay.

Q: What's the difference between a stagecoach and a basketball coach?
A: One runs roughshod over everything in its path, the other carries passengers.

Hoping to coast through his studies, the college basketball star signed up for math. When a friend asked him why, he said, "I've always been good with tools."

"Tools?"

"Yeah. I heard the toughest thing I gotta do is polish off some multiplication table."

The parents of the basketball star stormed into the dean's office.

"We want our kid out of this terrible school," said the mother.

"But why?" the dean asked. "He's in the top third of his class."

The father said, "That's what makes us think it's a terrible school."

The coach of the losing college team felt his ulcer acting up, so he scrawled "Back in an hour" on a sheet of paper, taped it to his office door, and went out to get a bite to eat.

When he returned, he found the following note scribbled beneath his: "What on earth for?"

The coach was a tyrant, and during a break the center said to a teammate, "Y'know, I feel like tellin' the coach to go to hell again."

"*Again?* What're you talking about?"

"I also felt like that yesterday."

The Pole walked up to the ticket booth.

"I know what you're thinking," he said to the clerk. "What the hell is this dumb Polack coming here for? He probably doesn't know the Knicks from the Celtics, and even if he does, he probably couldn't tell you which is the backboard and which is the foul line, or distinguish between a pick and a stuff. Well, I'll have you know that you won't be making fun of me! I'm one Polish fan who knows his stuff!"

"Excuse me," said the clerk, "but this is Yankee Stadium."

Then there was the sports buff who hated basketball on the TV. Claimed there wasn't enough room to do a lay-up.

Q: Where do the tallest members of a team go to find justice?
A: Center court.

Then there was the Polish cleaning woman who died while ironing the Celtics championship banners. She slipped and fell from the rafters.

Q: What was the prevailing emotion at the Knicks' home court when they blew an important game?
A: It was a woes garden.

Q: What did the young fan do when he met Wilt Chamberlain?
A: He spoke up.

"So there I was," said the man from Charlotte, "in the middle of the jungle, armed only with my diary, pen, and a canteen. And suddenly, a lion bounded from the tall grasses and approached me."

"What did you do?" asked a rapt listener.

"Well," said the man, "I grabbed the pen and quickly wrote on my arm, 'The Hornets'll win the championship this year.' "

"And that saved you?"

"You bet it did! Not even a lion would swallow that."

Walt, the basketball nut, walked into the bar.

"This is the proudest day of my life," he said. "My kid just made the college team."

One patron asked, "NYU?"

Walt scowled, "And why not?"

Then there was the senator who suggested erasing the national deficit by charging refs a dollar for every bad call . . .

. . . and the tennis buff who went to a 76ers game because someone told her she simply *had* to see the incredible Julius Erving. . . . (say the name fast)

It took a full year, but the high-school coach finally managed to convince the board of education to spring for new uniforms. Unfortunately, the players had grown since their measurements were taken, and the fit was rather snug, especially in the crotch. Captain John Black was elected to break it to the coach as gently as possible.

"Coach," said John, "these uniforms are really nice—but there *is* one thing wrong with them."

The coach's eyebrows rose. "Oh?"

"Sir—it's like, you know that room next to the cafeteria?"

"What room?"

"The ballroom."

The coach said, "Son—there's no ballroom."

John said, "Yes, sir. And now that you mention it, that's what's wrong with these uniforms."

Q: What do Indiana's basketball team and harness racing horses have in common?

A: The latter pacers are all horses, the former only the back half.

Q: How are the L.A. Clippers like fine wine?

A: Both are accustomed to life in the cellar.

Q: How tall is Bill Russell?

A: So tall that when he bends down to tie his shoe, he tries to find something else to do while he's down there so the trip won't be a waste.

Q: What's the difference between Wilt Chamberlain and a large bloodhound?

A: Nothing. They're both big scenters. . . .

BODY BUILDING

Powerhouse Pete, one of the world's biggest and most intimidating weight lifters, lumbered into the crowded bar. Unable to find an empty seat, he grabbed skinny little Charlie by the neck, lifted him from a stool, flung him to the side, and sat down.

Now, Charlie wasn't strong, but he was proud. And despite the pleas from his friend Andy, he picked himself up, walked over to Pete, and tapped him on the shoulder.

"Excuse me, sir, but that's my seat."

The brawny body builder turned. "You want it, little man, you're gonna have to fight for it."

The crowd began to cheer him on and, encouraged, Charlie accepted Powerhouse's offer.

Amid whoops and cries, tables and chairs were moved aside so the men would have room for their bout. Bets were placed as the two men stripped to their shorts, and the bartender struck a pitcher with a spoon to start the fight.

In one fluid, blinding move, Powerhouse picked Charlie up, dropped him across his knee, then tied him up in a combination leg hold/bearhug. The bartender began counting to three.

Suddenly, Powerhouse literally rose into the air and flew across the room, landing on the other side of the bar. Charlie leaped to the brute's side, lay atop the barely conscious weight lifter, and easily held him to the count of three.

The crowd was astonished and mobbed the lanky hero.

Andy fought his way to his friend's side. "My God, Charlie, how'd you ever do *that*?"

"Nothing to it," said the young man. "While he had me all twisted up, I saw a pair of nuts hanging right in front of my face. Well, I didn't need an invitation. I just opened my mouth and bit down *hard*."

"Hell," said Andy, "you must've bitten *damn* hard to make Pete go flying like that."

"You don't know the half of it," Charlie said. "It's awesome the strength you muster when you bite your own nuts."

The international body-building competition was being held in the United States, and it brought muscular specimens from all over the world.

No one was more imposing than the Soviet Union's brutish Sergei Starik. After working out, he went back to his locker and, much to his dismay, discovered that his wallet was missing. Just then, one of the competition translators walked by, holding a young locker-room attendant by the back of the neck.

"You," said Sergei, "what's wrong?"

"I caught this boy going through one of the lockers," said the translator.

Sergei glared at the attendant, then balled his fist and held it to the youth's face. "Ask if was he who took my wallet?"

The translator told the youth what the Russian had said.

"Yes!" said the boy, trembling. "Tell him I took his wallet! It's in my car!"

"Well?" said Sergei.

The translator said, "He told me, 'I'll bet that ugly slab of raw Russian beef doesn't have the balls to hit me.' "

Examining himself in the mirror, body builder Vinnie Papa frowned.

"What's wrong?" asked a man working out beside him.

"Don't like the look of my abs. They need more definition."

"Couple months back, Schwarzenegger was here and used dumbbells instead of barbells—"

"Good idea," Vinnie said, and he went and got a pair from the rack. He lay on his back, lifted them—and screamed.

"Christ! I—I think I ripped a muscle."

"Yup," said the other man. "That's what happened to Schwarzenegger too."

Hans and Franz rarely imbibed. However, after failing to make the final round of the Mr. Olympic competition, they decided to drown their sorrows in alcohol.

They got drunk after the second scotch and were barely able to stand after the fourth.

In time, Hans announced that he had to go to the bathroom. Mustering all his considerable strength, he made his way to the back, relieved himself, and returned.

"Hans," said Franz, "I'm too weak! Would you please go for me as well?"

Always willing to oblige, Hans struggled back to the lavatory and returned a few minutes later.

"Hey, you bastard!" Hans snarled. "You didn't even have to go!"

Another body builder walked into a bar for a meeting with an advertising executive.

"What'll you have?" the waitress asked the executive. He ordered a fuzzy navel, after which she turned to the body builder. "And you, sir?"

"Miss," he said, "I'd sooner have intercourse with a whore than pollute my body with alcohol."

As the waitress was about to leave, the advertising executive tugged at her apron. "Miss, as long as there's a *choice* . . ."

Pulling his dog behind him, the young boy ran up to the world-famous body builder and asked for his autograph.

"That's a cute dog you have there," the weight lifter said, making conversation as he struggled to spell out his name.

"Thank you, sir. I wanted to call him Lincoln, but my dad said that'd be an insult to the president. So I wanted to call him Lou, after you, but my dad wouldn't let me do that either."

"Good for your dad."

The boy said, "He told me that'd be an insult to the dog."

"Yes, sir," said the body builder to a friend, "I do love getting in shape. In fact, I'd rather be here than at home, having dinner."

The friend said, "Wouldn't your wife be upset if she heard that?"

"Not at all," said the body builder. "She'd rather watch TV than cook."

Then there was the Polish weight lifter who went to the doctor to get a hernia transplant. . . .

"What makes you say that body builder is vain?" Matilda asked Guy.

Guy replied, "Every year, on his birthday, he sends his parents a congratulatory telegram."

Q: What do most men do when they see a naked woman body builder?
A: Dress her with their eyes.

The skunk walked into the gym, causing heads with no necks to turn.

"Just where do you think you're going?" asked a trainer.

"Gonna press some iron," answered the skunk.

"Yeah? And what about that stink?"

The skunk replied, "I'll just have to get used to it."

The lanky man walked into the gym with a handcart.

"Anybody here a gambling man?" the skinny fellow asked.

A brawny man with a buzz cut and glistening muscles lumbered over.

"I'm a gambling man," he said. "What's the game?"

The visitor said, "I'll bet you a C-note I can pull something around the gym that you can't."

The body builder snorted. "You're on, pea brain."

After the money had been given to a trainer, the slender man pointed to the handcart. "Get on."

Q: What do you call a skinny guy who makes smart-assed bets with weight lifters?
A: Late.

Then there was the sage who pointed out that if you want to work out with dumbbells, there's no place better than a gym.

Case in point: the teen body builder who spent his mornings in the gym, then came to school with no shirt on so he could show off his biceps. The principal called it a distraction and ordered him to come to school fully clothed. However, the body builder insisted that the constitution guaranteed his right to bare arms. . . .

"Didja hear about Stevie Steel?" Ramone asked his friend. "He ate one too many griddle cakes after his morning workout, and exploded."

"Really?" his friend replied. "That's so waffle!"

It was the Pole's first trip to the gym. Walking into the locker room, he sat on the bench to change and noticed a sign beside him that said WET PAINT.

So he did.

A body builder named Strange went to see his lawyer.

"I'd like to add something to my will," said the body builder. "I want my tombstone to read, 'Here lies a body builder who never used steroids.'"

"Why do you want it to say that?" the lawyer asked.

"So people'll know who's buried there."

"I don't follow—"

The body builder said, "They'll look down at the inscription and say, 'Hey . . . that's strange!'"

Q: What did the spotters decide to call their union?
A: Weight watchers.

"My God!" the man said on his first session with the trainer. "This gym is as hot as an oven!"

The trainer replied, "What'd you expect? This is where I make my bread."

Q: Why did the weight lifter enjoy going to singles' joints?
A: He liked picking up those bar belles.

Q: When does a musclebound lout become a body builder?
A: When he marries your daughter.

Then there was the body builder who rushed to the phone to dial 911 when a fight broke out at the gym. He gave up because he couldn't find the eleven. . . .

More successful was the weight lifter who joined the circus as a strongman. He was so good, in fact, that he carried the whole show.

Q: What do London police officers call their workouts?
A: Bobby building.

Q: What do they call long lines at the gym?
A: Lifting waits.

Q: What's hard-boiled and weighs 250 pounds?
A: Arnold Schwarzenegg.

Q: What's the difference between a body builder and someone who's about to dig into a plate of clams?
A: One's musclebound, the other musselbound.

Women body builders have one thing every man desires: bulging muscles.

Q: What's the difference between Samson and the first winner of the Mr. Universe title?
A: Nothing. Both brought down the house.

BOWLING

It was a Friday night, and Rabbi Hager was overcome with a powerful urge to go bowling. Finding himself a lane in a corner of the local alley, he proceeded to bowl a 300.

As he stood there after the last strike, he looked at the heavens and cried, "A perfect game . . . and I can't tell a soul!"

Luigi and Tony were bagging their balls after a night at the alley.

"God," said Luigi, "I'd love to be a professional bowler in the worst way!"

Tony replied, "Quit now, babe. You're almost there."

Later, Luigi went back alone to practice his game. While he was there, a man ambled over with a soda and watched him play.

Unnerved, Luigi threw several gutter balls. Finally, he walked over to the man and said,

"Listen, bub—only bowlers are allowed on the lane proper."

The man replied, "I won't tell if you don't."

"Notice anything new about my game?" one leaguer asked another.

The other nodded. "Polished your ball."

Brutowski asked his friend the priest to go bowling with him. Though the clergyman rarely partook of the sport, he decided to go along.

He bowled terribly, and to make things worse, Brutowski was constantly teasing him about his form, his constant fouling, his frequent gutter ball. Never once, however, did the priest lose his temper.

At the end of the third game, as they were changing their shoes, the clergyman said, "I'd like to do this again next week."

"Love to," said Brutowski.

"Only this time I want you to bring your parents."

"Sure . . . but why?"

The priest said, "I'd like to marry them before the game."

"Damn," Scott complained to a friend, "one of the guys on my league team just ran off with my wife."

"Don't worry," said the friend. "You'll find someone else."

"With a 245 average?"

Judy wept into the phone.

"Doris ... Melvin has left me."

"Oh, he's done that before and always returned," Doris said.

"Not this time."

"How can you be sure?"

Judy sobbed, "He took his bowling ball."

Joshua and Manny sat at the bar after their nightly bowling game.

"Manny, I hate to say this, but tonight's the last night I can play. My wife says I'm preoccupied, and she's making me give up the game."

"God, that's awful," Manny said.

Joshua sighed. "You're telling me? Y'know, for twenty years the two of us were happy as could be."

"What went wrong?"

Joshua answered, "We met."

Murray walked into the house, dejected.

"The orthopedist says I can't bowl," he told his wife.

"Oh," she replied, "he's seen you play?"

Small, wiry Stanley left his friend in the bowling-alley lounge and walked over to where big, brawny bowler Behemoth Burt was sitting.

"Hey Behemoth," said Stanley, "how'd you like to make a little wager?"

"What kind of wager, little man?"

Stanley said, "I'll bet you two grand that I can piss into your drink from three yards away and not get a drop anywhere else."

Behemoth said, "Y'mean, if you get so much as a drop outside the glass, I win?"

Stanley nodded. Each man gave $2,000 to an independent observer, after which Stanley opened his fly, removed his member, and proceeded to pee on the table, chair, and even on Burt—everywhere but in the glass.

When he was finished, Behemoth laughed and scooped up the money. "Well, that was an easy two grand. Tell me, little man. Why'd you make such a stupid bet?"

Zipping up his fly, Stanley said, "It wasn't stupid at all. I bet my friend at the table four Gs that I could piss on your table and you'd be happy about it."

Once a year, New York's championship bowling team went to Chicago for a national playoff. On the night before the game, team leader Heshy Stock went to a bar where he struck up a conversation with the man on the stool beside him.

The men had a great time and agreed to meet

in the same place the night before the next tournament.

The year passed, and though Heshy didn't expect the man to be at the bar, he went anyway. Much to his delight, the man was sitting there, waiting.

"I can't believe it," Heshy cried, pumping the man's hand. "You remembered! You came back!"

"Back?" the man said. "Who left?"

Q: In lieu of pins, what do they use in the annual tournament played in Jacksonville?
A: Alligators. You've heard, surely, of the Gator Bowl.

Q: What do they call the yearly contest held on the planet Krypton?
A: The Super Bowl.

Mohalley was about to go for a spare when someone behind him coughed.

He stopped in midstride and turned. "You through back there, putz?"

"Sure, asshole."

Ball in hand, Mohalley stalked over. "You take dat back, or I'm gonna flatten your head wit' dis ball."

The man looked from the ball to Mohalley. He snickered, then said loud enough for everyone to hear, "I reiterate what I said."

Mohalley wagged a finger. "I accept, an' let dat be a lesson to you."

Q: What's the one thing bigger than a bowler's appetite?
A: His belly.

Q: What's the last thing a Polish stripper removes?
A: Her bowling shoes.

Q: On Saturday nights, what do they call the parking lot outside the local lanes?
A: A balling alley.

Paddy and Clyde went bowling. Each time Paddy released the ball, he yelled, "Fore!"

By the fourth frame, Clyde's curiosity got the best of him.

"Paddy," he said, "why do you yell 'fore' each time you get up to bowl?"

Paddy replied, "I'm trying to learn another language."

Biff and his son walked up to the counter in the bowling shop.

"I'd like a ball for my boy," he said.

The clerk looked at the youth. "Sorry," he said. "We don't do trade-ins."

Then there was the young woman who gave up bowling for sex. She heard the balls were lighter, and you didn't have to wear shoes . . .

. . . and the entrepreneur who opened a combination bowling alley/basketball court and called it Alley Hoop. . . .

Championship bowler Bobby Waldman went to see his doctor about a broken foot.

"How'd you do that?" asked the medic.

"Well, it's like this. Nine years ago, when I was just starting out, I was bowling in the lanes of a man who had the most beautiful daughter in the world. One night, she came over and asked me if there was anything I wanted . . . anything at all. I told her no. Later, she gave me a ride home and asked me if I was sure there was nothing I wanted. I said no. She walked me to the door and began playing with the buttons on her blouse, then asked if I was absolutely *certain* there was nothing I wanted. I thanked her and said no."

The doctor frowned. "What does all that have to do with your damn foot?"

"Well, I was warming up before a match today, and suddenly I realized what she meant! I was so angry, I threw the ball down on my foot!"

Q: Why was the major league pitcher a failure
   as a bowler?
A: He kept throwing the ball overhand.

Even dumber was Dan, who had a splitting
headache and went to the bowling alley. His doctor had told him to go and rest someplace where
he could hear a pin drop.

Stephen walked in the door, so elated he could
barely speak.
"Honey, guess what? I came the closest I've
ever come to bowling a perfect 300 game!"
"Really?" she said. "What'd you get?"
He replied, "A seventy-three."

Q: What's the difference between the American
   Bowling Congress and the U.S. Congress?
A: The members of one throw the ball, while
   the others throw the bull.

Q: What's another difference?
A: One requires the entire pin, the other just
   the pinheads.

BOXING

He was known as Granite Gus because he could take any punishment a fighter could dish out. He finally got his shot at the heavyweight title, and it was a bruising fight.

After the eleventh round, he lumbered back to his corner, his nose crushed, one eye shut and the other one nearly closed, ears bloody, cheeks horribly black and blue and lumpy.

"You got 'im," his manager told him. "Just hold on a little longer."

"H-hold on!" the big guy blurted through swollen lips. "How c-can I hit him if I can hardly see?"

"Who said anything about hitting?" the manager replied. "Just the sight of you is starting to make him weak."

Q: What's the difference between an underendowed man and Mike Tyson?
A: It's no fun to screw around with either of them.

Q: What's the difference between a boxer and a
   prostitute?
A: One's good with the hooks, the other hooks
   with the goods.

Difficult as it is to believe, a fighter once sent
Tyson to the floor. Iron Mike tripped over him
on the way to his corner.

Q: Why did the post office decide not to issue
   stamps honoring world heavyweight champs?
A: They couldn't be licked.

Q: How can you tell when a boxer's a sure loser?
A: He sells advertising on the bottom of his shoes.

The heavyweight champ was strolling through
the city streets with his latest girlfriend when
they were accosted by a runt of a mugger. Much
to the girl's surprise, the legendary fighter simply gave the thief his wallet, then watched as
the mugger scurried away.

"I can't believe what I just saw!" the girl
exclaimed. "The heavyweight boxing champion
of the world just handed over his wallet to a
ninety-eight-pound weakling. Why didn't you
pound him through the street?"

The champ shrugged. "There was four grand
in my wallet, and I never fight for under two
million."

Q: What's the difference between a baseball pitcher and a boxer?

A: One gets a no-hitter, he's a success, while the other's a failure.

Q: What's the difference between an infant and a boxer?

A: The infant looks forward to a bust in the mouth.

"Jeez," the sports writer said, running up to the boxer, "I heard you broke your left hand!"

"I did."

"Do you think you'll ever fight again?"

"Sure," said the boxer, "I'll be all right."

Q: Why do boxers find it tough to make a living in the fundamentalist South?

A: Because there's no punching allowed below the Bible Belt.

Q: Why did the Mafia don call himself a "Pugilistic Engineer?"

A: Because he made his living fixing fights.

Even more bizarre than the don was Sammy Lawrence, who had an unbelievable rabbit punch. Unfortunately, they put him in the ring with people.

Reminiscing about his days as a Golden Gloves fighter, Michael Michaelson told the other members of the old-age home, "Yes, sir . . . bell'd ring, and I'd rush at my opponent. First a left cross'd come, then a right cross'd come, then another left'd come."

Michael fell silent.

"Then what?" asked an old woman.

"Then"—Michael sighed—"the Red Cross'd come."

"However," Michael went on, "there was one fight where I really had my opponent worried."

"Why was that?"

"He thought he'd killed me."

Bert and Ernie had been best friends for seventy years, and their favorite pastime was watching the fights in person or on TV.

One day, in a reflective mood, Ernie asked, "Wouldn't it be terrible if we died and found out there was no boxing in heaven?"

"That would be awful," Bert agreed, and the two men made a pact: Whichever of them died first would somehow come back and tell the other whether or not there was boxing beyond the Pearly Gates.

Sadly, Ernie died a few days later. While the grieving Bert stood by his grave, weeping, he heard a familiar voice coming from above.

"Bert . . . Bert, it's me. . . ."

He looked up, and to his surprise and delight, there was Ernie, hovering just beyond a tree and wearing a halo and wings.

"My God! Ernie! It's so good to see you!"

"Bert," said the angel, "I come with good news and bad news."

"Really? What's the good news?"

"There's boxing in heaven, Bert. All the greats are here ... Louis, Corbett ... all of them! And they're still fighting."

"That's terrific! So what's the bad news?"

"You and I have ringside seats to the Marciano–Sullivan fight this Saturday night."

Q: Why was Glass Jaw Gary always laughing at his opponents?
A: Because every punch knocked him silly.

"Did you hear?" said one ticket seller to another. "The challenger was held up on his way home from the fight last night!"

Said the other, "After the pounding he took, it's the *only* way he could've made it."

"Hurry!" a man said, running up to Danny. "Your mother-in-law insulted Mike Tyson and now fists are flying!"

"So?" said the man. "Why should I care what happens to Mike Tyson?"

Q: What has four eyes, three ears, two noses, and fifty teeth?

A: A boxer with spare parts.

Gorilla McGuirk was one step above an anthropoid. A bruiser, he was so intellectually dense that his trainers could only communicate with him by sign language. There was a signal for him to rise, to sit, to smile, to drink, and to start fighting.

Young fighter Ron Borst was brought in to spar with the powerhouse. As he stepped into the ring, he noticed the trainers going through motions, which Gorilla was imitating. When they threw an uppercut outside the ring, so did he. When they unleashed a series of jabs, Gorilla did likewise.

After a while, Ron stepped back and dragged his wristband across his sweaty brow. Much to his horror, he saw Gorilla charge him, rip off his gloves, and nearly beat him to death.

It took the boxer's trainers and every other fighter in the place to pull Gorilla away.

"Wh-what happened?" Ron asked from the side of his swollen mouth.

"You wiped your forehead. That means 'Screw you' in sign language."

The next day, badly bruised, Ron took a hot dog, stuck it behind his fly, and returned to the gym. He went to the locker, where Gorilla was getting dressed by imitating what his trainer was doing.

When the trainer left, Ron walked over. He took out a pocketknife, opened his fly, slashed the hot dog in two, then handed the knife to Gorilla.

The boxer looked at the knife, then dragged his arm across his forehead.

After reading another sad newspaper account of Mike Tyson's wild private life, one boxing fan said to another, "This kind of behavior is terrible. People should look up to sports heroes."

"People *do* look up to Mike," said the other. "Got no choice when he knocks 'em flat on their back."

The two crooked managers were fixing a big fight.

"So in the first round," said one, "my guy will hit yours with two jabs and then a left uppercut, and your man'll go down."

The other manager shook his head. "Make it the sixth round. I mean, the people are coming to see a *fight*."

The boxer went to see his doctor.

"You're still suffering from insomnia?" the doctor said.

"Yeah."

"And you tried counting sheep, like I suggested?"

"Yeah, but that only made it worse."

"How?" asked the doctor.

The pugilist said, "Right before I get to ten, I jump off the mattress."

The battered fighter staggered into his corner after the fourth round.

"I got a new strategy for you next round," his manager said. "Try hitting back."

Then there was the boxer who used his fame to preach the gospel part-time. He called himself a pewgilist.

After the one-sided fight, the loser's trainer ran over to a judge.

"You bastard!" he screamed. "My man didn't deserve a zero in that final round."

"I agree," said the judge. "Unfortunately, I'm not permitted to give anything lower."

The attendant at the insane asylum turned to the head doctor.

"Sir, a man on the phone wants to know if we had anyone escape recently."

"Why?"

"He says someone just ran up and popped Mike Tyson in the nose, then stood there laughing."

Q: What's the only thing thicker than a boxer's ears?
A: What's between them.

Q: Why couldn't the boxer light the campfire?
A: He had a habit of losing his matches.

After a devastating first round, the boxer stumbled into the corner. After tending to his wounds, his trainer said, "Jake, I think you misunderstood me."

"Wh-whaddya mean?"

The trainer replied, "When I said you should go out there and show him what you're made of, I didn't mean to let him knock the stuffing out of you."

Q: Why did the boxer only fight on weekends?
A: Because he regarded the sport as a part-time jab.

Q: What part of a boxing glove causes the most damage?
A: The outside.

Q: What's the difference between a losing boxer and a thirsty man at a party?
A: Someone beat them both to the punch.

Then there were the two gay boxers who got into the ring and exchanged blows.

Q: What word is most regularly heard during Mike Tyson's sparring sessions?
A: "Next!"

The heavyweight champion went to the bathroom in the lobby of a first-class hotel. As he left the stall, he noticed that the man handing out towels was a former contender.

Obviously enjoying the predicament of his one time rival, the champion grinned and laid a hundred-dollar bill on the man's tray.

"Brutus," said the champ, "I always wondered where you disappeared to. Things musta gotten pretty rough for you to be doin' this."

Drawing himself up proudly, the former fighter said, "Actually, the tips are great and business is booming. Dozens of pisses have been passed here today"—he looked up pointedly—"though I must admit you're the first shit I've seen so far."

Q: In which motion picture does a famous cinematic boxer take on a geological landmark?
A: Rocky Mountains.

Q: In which motion picture does that same boxer die and pass through the Pearly Gates?
A: *Rocky Seven.* (say it fast. . . .)

After brawling in a local bar, the boxer was brought before a judge.

"Your honor," said the fighter's attorney, "my client is charged with disturbing the peace ... but the fact is, he's a boxer. He was simply practicing his craft."

"I see," said the judge. "In that case, I sentence your client to 9,000 rounds in prison."

When the sentence was pronounced, the lawyer tried another tack.

"Your Honor," he said, "I don't think you understand. My client is not responsible for what happened. His arms have their own will, their own minds. Even if his brain says no, they involuntarily jab, jab, jab—he can no more stop them from working than he can stop his heart from beating."

"I understand and I sympathize," said the judge. "I sentence your client's arms to prison. He can accompany them or not, as he chooses."

Q: He may have been the Greatest, but who was also the most egocentric boxer in history?
A: All I.

Q: What was the difference between Sonny Liston and an ancient potter?
A: One pounded Clay, and Clay pounded one.

While Willie was giving the heavyweight champ a rubdown, he said, "Say—how's that girlfriend of yours?"

"Janet? She got the clap and bled to death."

Willie said, "I don't get it. People don't bleed to death from the clap."

The champ replied, "They do when they give it to me."

Q: What's Mike Tyson's favorite song?
A: "The Beat Goes On."

The referee stared aghast as the heavyweight contender stumbled into the ring, clearly drunk.

"Take him back to his dressing room and don't let him out till he's sober," the official ordered his trainer.

"It looks like we've got a problem then," said the trainer. "He won't fight Tyson if he's sober."

Then there was the trainer who offered this observation about the sport: "The only thing all boxers have in common is that no two of 'em fight the same."

Shortly after 3:00 A.M., there was a pounding at the door of fight promoter Ron King.

"Who the hell is it?" King shouted out the window.

"Arnie Belnick," came the reply. "Are you the man who offered a million bucks to anyone who could go three rounds with Killer Conroy?"

"Yes—"

"Well, I just wanted to let you know that I'm not gonna take you up on it."

Hurting for business, the gym offered fighters sparring partners at no extra charge. Or, as the sign outside read FREE ALTERCATIONS!

The proprietor of the gym also announced a grand reopening, with free drinks and fistivities.

Q: What's the difference between a bad boxer and a streetwise kid?
A: Nothing. They both know all the ropes.

Q: What's the best way to get a bloody nose before a junior welterweight bout?
A: Go over and Hector Camacho.

Two birds were pecking at a piece of bread outside Madison Square Garden.

"Say," said one, "are you for Cooney in tonight's fight?"

"Why do you ask?"

Replied the bird, "Because I understand he's for us."

Q: What do Mike Tyson and Michael Jackson have in common?

A: They both make their living by delivering hits.

After being rejected by several young studs on the beach, a rather flat-chested young woman was walking alone when she stumbled across a dirty old lamp. She picked it up, rubbed off the sand, and was amazed when smoke spiraled from the oil well. It solidified into a magnificent man dressed in a turban.

"I am the great genie of Aladdin," it boomed. "Make a wish and I will grant it!"

The woman glanced back at the men frolicking in the surf with the big-bosomed beauties. "Genie—I'd like the two biggest boobs on earth."

"Granted," he said, and the woman was instantly enveloped in smoke.

When the shroud lifted, Mike Tyson and Leon Spinks were standing beside her.

Marvin Hagler and an opponent were playing the crowd at their weigh-in.

"When I hit a foe," the rival warned, "he *remembers* it!"

Unfazed, Hagler replied, "That's nothin'. When I hit a foe, he *stops* rememberin'!"

Q: What's the difference between a skier and a boxer?
A: The skier doesn't mind going to Zermatt.

Q: What's the difference between a man with a cold and a boxer?
A: One blows his nose, the other knows his blows.

Then there was the former basketball center who became a prizefighter and developed cauliflower navel . . .

. . . and the crooked fighter who took dives for big bucks. The only time his bouts were clean was when his trainer threw in the towel. . . .

Q: When fighting Marvin Hagler, what's more important than presence of mind?
A: Absence of body.

Then there was the young lady who dated Hagler for the first and last time. While suggesting places they could go, she asked, "Have you ever been to the zoo? As a visitor, I mean?"

Q: What's the difference between a beautiful woman and a Hagler opponent?
A: One has a face that's striking, the other a face that's struck.

Q: Why are boxers a paradox?
A: Because the weakest part of their body is protected by the thickest.

Then there was the boxer who took so many punches in the cheeks that only an electric shaver could get in all the crevices. You might say he had a face only a motor could love....

Another unlucky boxer had his nose broken in two places. He's never going back to either one of them again.

Q: What's the difference between a dirty shirt and a highly publicized fight that lasts less than a round?
A: One has ring around the collar, the other has choler around the ring.

FISHING

Q: What's the definition of a dumb fisherman?
A: Someone who's out fishing with his girl-friend, is asked to hand her a rod, and gives her a fishing pole.

Q: Why do most women prefer fishing to sex?
A: Not as boring.

Shep Boucher was a notorious man-about-town, and his wife Tillie was sick of his womanizing. She told her neighbor Madge that the next time he came in late, she was going to storm out.

One night, Madge heard Shep's car pull into the driveway at midnight. Much to her surprise, Tillie didn't appear.

The next day, Madge phoned Tillie and asked why she hadn't left.

"Because the big lug said he'd been fishing," Tillie told her.

"But I saw him come in. He didn't have any fish."

Tillie replied, "That's why I believed him."

The warden walked up to the young man.

"You'll have to leave," said the warden. "You need a license to fish here."

"Like hell I do," said the young man. "I'm doing swell with worms."

As they put the rowboat into the water, Roger told his son, "Boy—always remember, there are two types of people who fish. Those who fish for sport, and those who catch something."

Warren came ashore where his wife was waiting for him. Embarrassed by the fact that he hadn't caught a thing, he said, "Hon—you should've seen the one that got away. It fought me for three hours—musta been seventy, eighty pounds if it was an ounce."

His wife looked over at him. "Warren, one of the kids on the beach loaned me his binoculars. That fish you were fighting wasn't even as long as your foot."

Unfazed, Warren said, "Hell, you must've looked in at the end of the fight. Incredible how much weight those rascals can lose in a few hours!"

"I'm confused," Steve said as he and his friend Tom sat in the boat, fishing. "I've got a more expensive rod, I use the best lures, and I have years more experience than you. But you always seem to catch more fish. What gives?"

Tom said, "I have a system. When I get up in the morning, if my wife's sleeping on her right side, I fish the right side of the boat. If she's on her left side, I fish off the left side."

"What do you do if she's on her back?"

Tom grinned. "Then I don't go fishing."

Then there were the Poles who went ice fishing. They drowned while frying their catch.

Kelsey was such an avid fisherman and his collection of equipment so unparalleled that his wife was at a loss as to what to do with it when he died. Fortunately, her lawyer was able to sell it off for a tidy profit, making him the world's first reel-estate agent. . . .

Then there was the fish that found itself hooked and struggled with baited breath.

More successful were the two fish who were carefully picking apart lures to upset fishermen and muttering, "Time's sure fun when you're having flies!"

The fastest-growing thing in nature is a fish. Its growth is incredible between the time you catch it and the time you tell someone about it.

"Holy mackerel," one fish said breathlessly to another, "you should've seen the size of the guy that nearly caught me! Big as a house, he was. . . ."

Dee Child was a little girl who loved fishing more than anything, especially school. She'd set off for the little red schoolhouse each morning, but as soon as she passed the creek she'd stop, take out the rod she kept hidden in a tree, and plant herself on the cozy bank.

One day during lunch, Dee's teacher went out looking for her. He found the girl, brought her home, and suggested that her mother break the pole and punish her daughter.

Dee's mother softened when her daughter began to cry, and she let her keep the pole. The next day, Dee set out for school ... and once again ended up at the creek.

The moral: Spare the rod and spoil Dee Child.

Harold was hauled into court for catching twenty fish at a lake where the limit was strictly five.

"How do you plead?" asked the judge.

"Guilty as hell, Your Honor."

"I fine you $500."

"Thank you," said Harold, "but you'd better tack on another fifty cents."

"And why is that?"

Harold replied, "Because I want copies of the court record to show my friends."

Q: What do they call it when atomic scientists grab their rods and gather around the old watering hole?
A: Nuclear fishin'.

After a day on the lake, Theodore stopped at the fish market.

"Jimmy, toss me three trout," he said to the owner.

"You want me to *throw* 'em?"

"That's right. I want to be able to tell me wife I caught them."

Young Woodrow shambled into Sunday school.

"Why are you late?" the teacher asked.

"I had a fight with my dad. He wouldn't let me go fishing."

"That's very commendable," the teacher said. "And did he tell you *why* you couldn't fish today?"

"Yes," said Woodrow. "He said there was only enough bait for one of us."

After listening to her husband's tale of the huge marlin he tangled with and lost, the woman looked behind him and said, "Here comes Batman!"

"Batman?" her husband said.

She smiled. "He must've heard the Joker was in town."

Then there was the psychotic young man who went from lake to river killing fish. His name? Norman Baits . . .

Quentin listened patiently, tongue in his cheek, while his friend Alex described his weekend fishing off Montauk, during which he allegedly tangled with a fifty-foot-long shark.

When Alex was finished, he asked Quentin, "How was your weekend in Maine?"

"I'll tell you," Quentin said, "you wouldn't believe the whales you attract when you use a great white as bait. . . ."

After sitting on the rowboat for three hours without so much as a nibble, Mark turned to Bernie.

"I thought you said this was a great place for fish."

"It is," said Bernie. "Notice how they refuse to leave it?"

After rowing along the river and its tributaries for three days, the two campers had to admit they were lost. There wasn't another soul in sight, and they were at a loss as to what to do.

"How many fish have we caught today?" one of the men asked.

"Six."

"What's the limit?"

"Ten."

The man broke out his rod. "Catch five more. The warden'll find us before we've reeled 'em in."

Flo came back to Warren's apartment. As they entered the den, she started: there, on the wall, was a thirty-foot-long great white.

"Caught him when I was out fishing with my dad a few years back," Warren said proudly.

Flo hesitantly touched the shark's rough hide. "It's so realistic," she said. "What's it stuffed with?"

Warren replied, "Dad."

Peter was the worst fisherman on earth, bar none. Each weekend during the summer he'd go out on the boat with his friends, and each weekend he'd come back empty-handed.

One weekend, he decided to break the losing streak. Instead of packing a fishing rod, he packed a semiautomatic machine gun.

Peter's friends felt for him, and though the roar was sure to scare away the fish, his self-esteem was more important.

Driving out to the river, they pulled on their boots, waded out, and began casting. Peter stood up to his waist in the water, gun at the ready, eyes scanning the water.

Suddenly, he saw a trout. Raising his gun, he aimed and fired. Bullets splat against the water, then all was still ... until the fish could be seen swimming briskly by.

Trying to put a good face on yet another disaster, Peter cried, "Go on and swim, damn you! Swim with your friggin' fish heart shot out!"

Then there was the young nurse who hated fishing, but loved going down on the doc ...

... and the Pole who went ice fishing, then couldn't convince his friends he'd caught a fifty-pounder. The stuff melted before he got it home. ...

Q: What was written on the sign the Pole attached to his line?
A: THIS END IN.

Dirk and Kirk were sitting in their rowboat in the middle of a lake.

After two hours, Kirk crossed his legs. Two hours later, he uncrossed them.

Dirk glowered at him. "Dammit, man, did you come here to fish or do aerobics?"

As they were fishing on the lake, the little boy asked his somewhat senile grandfather, "Pops, how do you make a boat float?"

The old man said, "With a boat, seltzer, and a scoop o' ice cream."

Q: What's the most important thing to have when ice fishing?
A: Excellent ice site.

The sheriff approached the kid who was fishing by the lake.

"Say, boy, can't you read that sign?" the law officer snapped. "Says, 'No Fishing Allowed.'"

The boy turned and whispered, "I'm fishing very quietly, sir."

The kid asked, "Ma, can I go out fishing?"
"What? With those holes in your shoes?"
"No, with my fishing pole."

The kid managed to go fishing, then came running home.

"Ma, I saw a catfish down at the dock!"

"Really," she replied. "How did it hold the fishing pole?"

Julio was about to go on vacation when he realized he'd forgotten his fishing rod. Rather than go home, he stopped at a sporting-goods store.

"I'd like to buy a fishing rod," Julio said, "and be quick about it! I've got to catch a plane."

The clerk shrugged. "I'll sell you a rod, but I'll be damned if I know what lure to suggest."

Q: What's the difference between a kid who loathes reading and a fisherman?
A: One hates books. . . .

Fenwick, the world's worst fisherman, was gravely ill. Mrs. Picot came to the hospital to visit.

"How is he?" she asked.

"He's lying at death's door," said the physician.

Mrs. Picot shook her head. "About to meet his maker and *still* lying."

But Fenwick recovered, and frustrated by the fact that his license had expired, he went fishing anyway.

Caught by the game warden, he was dragged into court.

"You're charged with catching a trout. How do you plead?"

"Not guilty, Your Honor," said Fenwick. "I took it for a lark."

"I see," the judge replied. "Well, thirty days in jail will give you plenty of time to learn the difference between scales and feathers."

Q: What's the difference between a game warden and a tetanus shot?
A: None. They're both a pain in the ass.

Q: What do they call fish caught by black anglers?
A: Sole food.

Then there was Mr. Quint, who was asked to go freshwater fishing and promised to mullet over . . .

. . . and the fisherman who invented fake, radio-controlled fish for hapless anglers. He called it a plastic sturgeon. . . .

Amos and a pal were fishing when Amos accidentally dropped his wallet into the bay. As he reached down and tried to grab it, a carp knocked the wallet away. Amos watched helplessly as another carp came by and nosed it even farther from shore. A collision with a third carp sent the wallet down and out of sight.

"I'll be damned," said Amos. "That's the first time I've ever seen carp-to-carp walleting."

Q: What part of the fish do most fishermen end up bringing home?
A: The tale.

Q: What did the Irish Mexican say when the fish ripped up his fly?
A: "Tore a lure, ole!"

Q: What did the fisherman do to entertain his little nephew on the boat?
A: Cod tricks.

Q: How do Polish fishermen count the day's catch?
A: "One fish, two fish, another fish, another fish, another . . ."

Q: When is a fisherman like a football player?
A: When he's a lyin' man.

Then there was the only flatfish that managed to escape the fishermen's nets. Though sad at losing its comrades, the fish was grateful to have been the sole survivor. . . .

As it happens, the fish wasn't alone for long. A priest compelled the fishermen to free their catch, insisting that God had commanded him to go forth and save soles. . . .

Q: How did the methodical caviar merchant make sure he didn't miss a single fish egg?
A: He went after them roe by roe.

Gary had it all planned. He rented a boat, took his wife out to sea, did a little fishing, then began to seduce her on the deck, beneath a starlit sky.

Unfortunately, while his wife was undressing, she slipped on a fish they'd caught, hurt herself, and had to go below. It was just another example of sex being called off because of a haddock.

Q: What do politicians and fish have in common?
A: As soon as they open their mouths, they get in trouble.

Morey came upon his niece Estelle sitting by the pool. She was holding a cue stick, its tip in the water.

"What are you doing?" he asked.

"Fishing," she replied.

Morey smiled. "What kind of fish do you think you're going to catch in there—and with a cue stick, no less?"

Without missing a beat, she replied, "A pool shark."

Q: What do you call an egocentric angler?
A: Someone who's me-deep in water.

Q: When is the fishing always best?
A: Before you get there and after you leave.

After a day of great fishing, the two Poles decided to rent a boat again the following day.

"But how will we know exactly where to come?" asked one, looking around the vast lake.

The other took a scaling knife from his pocket and scraped an X on the bottom of the boat. "Now we'll know to come right back here," he said.

His companion frowned. "Don't be an ass! What if we get a different boat?"

As they were rowing back to shore, one Pole looked at their catch and asked the other, "Which fish do you think have their eyes closest to their mouths?"

The other thought for a while, then said, "The smallest ones."

Then there was the fisherman who couldn't catch a thing, so he stole fish from another angler. His motto was to feed his family by hook or by crook. . . .

Another man was such an avid fisherman that he even enjoyed getting packages COD.

Q: What do you call a big defensive football player who enjoys angling?
A: A fishing tackle.

Two Poles were out fishing, and not only weren't the fish biting, but the mosquitoes were awful.

"Let's stay until night," said one of the men. "Maybe the fish will come out and the mosquitoes will go home."

The men sat on the shore until well after sunset, at which point the bugs left and the fish began biting. However, one of the men suddenly rose.

"Forget it," he said, "I'm going home."

"Why?"

He pointed to tiny flecks of light in the air around them. "Because the little bastards are back, and they're looking for us with flashlights."

Then there was the fisherman who didn't get a single bite, but had plenty of nips. . . .

Q: How does the former Cincinnati baseball manager get out to his favorite spot on the lake?
A: Pete rows.

Q: Why does he always go with former slugger Carew?
A: It'd be dull with no Rod.

Q: Why did the fisherman decide to abandon a lifelong habit of skipping church?
A: He misunderstood his wife. He *thought* she said the priest would be sermonizing about how it's okay if everyone loafs and fishes.

Q: What do you call a bit of doggerel written by a fisherman?
A: Mackerel.

Q: What do you call a fish that plays Chopin?
A: A piano tuna.

Finally, though the pole didn't have a license, he saw no problem with taking out his gear and trying his luck at the lake. After all, the sign *did* say *Fine for Fishing*.

FOOTBALL

Not-so-bright Dan went to a Giants game with his girlfriend Tish.

As they were sitting there, enjoying the game, a bird few overhead and deposited droppings on the young lady's head.

Dan continued watching the game, and Tish grew livid.

"Don't just sit there!" she screamed. "Go and get some toilet tissue!"

"What for?" Dan asked. "That bird's long gone."

Jack and Alice were having dinner with friends when they were told about a mutual acquaintance, who tried to trade his wife for season tickets on the fifty-yard line to Buffalo games.

"That's horrible!" shrieked Alice. "Don't you try to do anything like that, Jack."

"Don't be silly," Jack replied. "The Bills are having a lousy season!"

There's a rumor about the linebacker who was so ugly that the doctor slapped the baby's mother when he was born. . . .

Then there was a horseman from Indiana who bought a pair of young stallions from a trader in New Delhi. The trader made sure to send over a supply of their favorite apples as well; without them, the animals would soon grow homesick and die.

Unfortunately, the shipment of apples was lost, and before the owner could procure any more, the two animals wasted away and died.

The moral: You'll always lose money on the Indian, appleless colts.

Q: What's the toughest challenge most pro linemen ever face?
A: Graduating the sixth grade.

Jets wide receiver Winston LeRoy was jogging through the streets of Manhattan one morning when he saw a crowd gathered below an apartment building. He looked up and saw a woman standing on the ledge of a fifth-floor window. She was clutching a baby to her bosom as smoke churned from the room behind her.

Winston began running toward the building.

"Hey, lady!" he shouted. "Throw me the kid!"

"No!" she cried. "It—it's a five-story drop!"

"Don't worry," he yelled back, "I play for the Jets! I'll catch him!"

Flames kissed the woman's feet and, reluctantly, she heaved the baby toward the street.

The crowd parted as Winston ran forward. The athlete extended his arms, and his sharp eyes never left the precious bundle as it tumbled gently past each floor.

He poured on the speed, adjusted his approach as the wind carried the baby toward the street. The child passed the second floor, the first floor—

Winston stretched and felt the infant on his fingertips. He took a mighty step to get his hands fully beneath the babe. The precious bundle settled into his palms and he quickly hauled the baby to his chest.

The crowd roared and applauded and, without thinking, the big man lifted the baby above his head and spiked it.

College coach Higgins was sitting in his office when he saw a small, nerdy student run past his door. A moment later, his star tackle Joseph went barreling past, stark naked and dripping wet.

Higgins called after him, and Joseph put on the brakes. The coach walked over to his glowering player.

"You're supposed to be in the whirlpool nursing that leg, Joseph. Just what the hell do you think you're doing?"

"Sorry, coach, but that little shit just stole one o' my shoelaces."

"So? We've got more."

Joseph started after the nerd. "I know. But first I gotta find out which shoe he took it from."

Then there was the football player *so* dumb that he had to be told to put on a clean athletic supporter for every game. Unfortunately, midway through the season, he couldn't get his pants on over them.

The good news about the rookie placekicker was that he could hit a field goal from his own thirty-yard line. The bad news was that he could only do it in the nude, which limited his appearances to exhibition games.

Then there was the tackle who was so dumb he thought his sexual organs were in his fingers: more than once, he heard the opposing team warn their quarterback, "He gets his hands on you, you're screwed."

Q: What's a typical fan's definition of football?
A: A game that takes four quarters to go through a fifth.

Q: What does Jim Brown have in common with an athletic supporter?

A: Both are reliable ball carriers.

Q: And how did teenagers in Cleveland get dates on a Saturday night?

A: They stood outside Jim Brown's window.

The seat beside Jim at the Redskins playoff game was empty.

During halftime, Jim said to the man on the other side, "Pretty incredible to have a no-show at a game like this."

The man said, "That's my wife's seat."

"I see," said Jim. "She sick?"

"No. She's dead."

"Oh," said Jim, "I'm sorry. Couldn't you find a friend or relative to come with you?"

"Uh-uh," said the man. "They're all at her funeral."

Then there was the fan who really infuriated the spectators in the row below him. He drank so much beer and got so drunk that when the cheerleaders yelled, "Go! Go! Go!", he did.

Q: Who's the one man no college football program in the nation could survive without?

A: The kid who takes the tests for the players.

Q: How is a billionaire's son like a return specialist?

A: You don't receive until someone kicks off.

Q: How do high-school coaches in Alabama determine who should be backs and who should be linemen?

A: They send the hopefuls running at a brick wall. Those who go around it are backs. Those who go through it are linemen.

Then there was the pro coach who decided to travel with a gorilla. That way, when any of his players got injured, he'd have spare parts.

Q: Why was the quarterback the one member of the college team who managed to graduate?

A: No one else could pass.

Q: Why was the playboy quarterback fearful of having knee surgery?

A: He was told it might make him limp.

Eustace Lee was admitted to Yale on a football scholarship. Lost on his first day of school, he stopped a professor while crossing the campus and said, " 'Scuse me, but d'you know where the library's at?"

The elderly teacher looked at the youth with disdain, rankled that the school had compromised its standards and admitted a student solely for sports.

"Young man," said the professor, "don't you know that one never ends a sentence with a preposition?"

The student cleared his throat. " 'Scuse me, but d'you know where the library's at, asshole?"

Q: Why do football players wear helmets?
A: So they don't wipe the wrong end.

The hypercompetitive young quarterback was feeling under the weather and reluctantly went to see the medic.

The doctor took his temperature, then looked down at the thermometer.

"You've got the flu," he said, "which is no surprise, considering how you're always pushing yourself. If we don't get this fever down, you won't be playing on Sunday."

"How high is it?" asked the quarterback.

"You've got 102."

"I see," said the athlete. "Just out of curiosity, what's the team record?"

The university coach was being interviewed by sportscasters, and sick and tired of hearing about how dumb football players are, he cited a survey he'd recently read.

"According to a Canter Poll, over half of the young men who play college ball are making *A*s and *B*s."

"That's wonderful," said a cynical interviewer. "The question is, when will they learn to write the rest of the alphabet?"

All-star college running back Larry Lawrence was failing miserably in every subject, so the dean went to the coach with an ultimatum: Lawrence could play in the big game only if he could learn and remember the formula for water.

That seemed fair to the coach, who enlisted the science teacher to sit and drill the gridiron star for several hours every day.

On the morning of the game, the dean came to the coach's office, where Lawrence sat with a big smile on his face.

"Ready?" asked the dean.

"Ready," said the coach.

The dean looked over at Lawrence. "So, my friend: what's the formula for water?"

Without hesitation, the big tackle drew back his shoulders and said, "H-I-J-K-L-M-N-O."

Larry's teammate, quarterback Robbie Roberts, didn't have much more luck. Informed that he couldn't play in the book game unless he passed his math test, he took his textbook and notes and sequestered himself in his room all week.

On the day of the exam, Robbie felt good. He walked into the classroom, accepted the examination book from the professor, then stepped into the pocket and threw it smack into the teacher's arm.

The less-than-brilliant football player sat heavily on the bar stool, his expression gloomy.

"Hey, why so down?" the bartender asked. "I read that you just got engaged."

"Nah . . . it's off," said the player.

"That's too bad. What happened?"

"She admitted she loved another man."

"No kidding—"

"No. Last night, she told me she'd be true to the end."

The bartender scratched his head. "What's wrong with that?"

"I'm the quarterback."

After a tiring day of watching football on TV, Ivan fell asleep in his easy chair. Instead of waking him, his wife let him sleep and went to bed.

The next morning, she found her husband still snoozing in his chair.

Nudging him gently, she said, "Wake up, dear. It's twenty to seven."

Ivan started, and yelled, "Whose favor?"

Q: Behind several touchdowns, why did the coach send in his second string?
A: In a desperate effort to tie the game.

The boy and his father were watching a football game on TV.

"Dad, what do quarterbacks do when their eyes go bad and they can't think on their feet anymore?"

"Why, that's simple, son. They become referees."

The high-school football player walked into the house after practice.

"How'd you do today, son?" his father asked.

"I made an eighty-five-yard run—"

"Hey, that's great!"

"No, it stinks. I never did catch the guy I was running after."

Then there was the kid who broke his finger playing football with a busted pay phone. He was trying to get the quarter back. . . .

Q: What's a quarterback's least-favorite dessert?
A: Turnovers.

No sooner had Bennett sat down than his wife stormed into the den and stood in front of the TV, blocking his view of the football game.

"Bennett," she said, "I swear, I'd drop dead if just *once* you said you wanted to spend Sunday's with me!"

Bennett replied, "Don't tempt me."

The next day, Bennett was having lunch with a co-worker.

"My wife says either I give up football or she's leaving," Bennett said.

"What're you going to do?" asked the co-worker.

"Well," said Bennett, "I'll miss her at first. . . ."

Bennett's wife reneged, allowing her husband to watch football . . . though she did put her foot down as far as their social life was concerned.

"Look," she said, "I want to enjoy my high-school reunion, so do me a favor and *don't* talk about football. It's dull. You can talk politics, you can talk about women, you can even talk about religion . . . but *no* football. Agreed?"

Bennett agreed, though as the reunion got under way he knew it was going to be difficult. He pressed his lips together and breathed deeply through his nose, trying to think of anything but football.

A couple walked over and began chatting with Bennett and his wife.

"Say," the man said to Bennett after a few minutes, "you haven't said a word. Is everything okay?"

Bennett nodded.

"You sure?" the man pressed.

And Bennett blurted, "Tell me—do you think Joe Montana believes in God?"

One Sunday afternoon, a man walked into a bar in Boston. He was carrying a small dog under his arm. After ordering, he and the dog retired to a table to watch the New England Patriots play the Jets.

During the fourth quarter, the Pats finally got onto the board, scoring a field goal. Immediately, the dog began to whoop and dance.

"Way to go!" the animal shouted as he stood on his hind legs and did a little jig. "Nice job, guys!"

Everyone in the bar watched the performance, and when it was finished, the bartender said, "What the heck kind of dog *is* that?"

"Oh, he's a real New England fan. He does that every time they score."

"Christ," said the bartender, "what does he do when they win?"

"I wouldn't know," said the customer. "I've only had him four years."

Q: What do you get when you cross a parrot with Refrigerator Perry?

A: I've no idea, but when it talks, you'd better listen.

Q: What did they call the Atlanta footballer who drank only tea purchased at the Peachtree shopping center?

A: The mall-teas Falcon.

Q: Why did the owner of the L.A. Rams insist that all the players wear necklaces?

A: So that when the fans pointed to the chokers, they wouldn't take it personally.

The coach cared deeply for his players. He especially hated telling draftees they hadn't made the team and came up with the kindest way he could think of to break the news.

"Sorry," he'd say, greeting them at the door, "but visitors aren't allowed in the locker room."

Another coach cared more about winning, and when his team found itself three points down, he went right to the second string.

"Awright, Grabowski," he said to one of the players, "you go out there and get serious."

"Right," said Grabowski. "What's his number?"

Then there was the player who hurt himself, went to the chiropractor, and demanded a big discount because he was a quarterback. . . .

That same quarterback had had a long college career—nine years, to be exact. It took him a long time to learn how to pass.

After a call of intentional grounding, the quarterback shouted at the ref, "Mister—you stink!"

The ref penalized the team fifteen yards for the outburst, then asked, "Can you still smell me?"

"No," the man said to his wife, "watching football isn't a matter of life and death. It's more important than that."

One of the Dallas cheerleaders wasn't feeling well, and she went to see the team physician. After stripping and lying facedown on his examination table, she cried, "Doctor! You've put the thermometer in the wrong hole!"

"It's not the wrong hole," he replied, "and it's not the thermometer."

Actually, the team physician was something of a quack. He devised a special painkiller for the players: one part aspirin to ten parts pot. The theory was that if it didn't cure what ailed the players, they'd be in no condition to complain.

In time, a new team physician was hired, and the quarterback went to see him.

"Doc," he said, "it's terrible. The coach'll send in plays from the sidelines, and as soon as I've heard 'em, I forget 'em."

"Short-term memory loss," the doctor said. "How long have you had this problem?"

The quarterback said, "What problem?"

A play is something that takes seconds for players to execute and minutes for fans to describe.

Sick and tired of the general manager's advances, the cheerleader found employment elsewhere. Then she went to his office and boldly announced, "I've got a new position."

"Great!" said the GM, undoing his pants. "Let's try it!"

When the injured player returned to the squad, a teammate asked, "At which joint was your surgery done?"

The player replied, "Listen, bub, don't you speak about that hospital with disrespect."

Discussing the quarterback's injury, the coach said to the general manager, "I'm afraid our boy's going to be in there quite awhile."

"You've seen his doctors?" asked the GM.

"No," said the coach. "His nurses."

Then there was the brilliant quarterback who only had one problem: Every time he looked at the fearsome front four of the opposing team, he wet himself.

Though he hoped no one noticed, he was extremely self-conscious as he ran to the sidelines to confer with the coach during a time out.

"You're in trouble," the coach said, glancing at the clock.

Blushing, the quarterback replied, "Exactly."

It was halftime, and while a high-school band was marching on the field one of the TV cameramen accidentally dropped a cigarette into a stack of cables.

As the insulation smoldered, a drunk in the front row sniffed, then shouted out to the bandleader, "Hey, dude, you're marchin' those kids too damn fast!"

Q: What do you call a short pass from an AC/ DC QB?
A: Bilateral.

Q: Which player does this quarterback go to most often?
A: He prefers a tight end.

Q: How much does it cost Refrigerator Perry to see a shrink?
A: A hundred dollars for the hour, $500 for the couch.

Q: Why doesn't Refrigerator wear yellow anymore?
A: He got tired of people yelling, "Taxi!" when he walked by.

Q: What has eight legs, is white and green, and has an IQ of sixteen?
A: The Eagles' front four.

One Atlanta Falcons cheerleader said to the other, "Y'know, horny players are all alike!"

The other grinned and said, "Horny players are all ah like too!"

Q: Why do the Giants drink Gatorade instead of Kool-Aid?
A: Because they can't get two quarts of water into those small packets.

Q: How many Dallas players does it take to change a light bulb?

A: Three. The center to snap it, the quarterback to do the changing, and the coach to tell him how.

Q: How many Indianapolis players does it take to change a light bulb?

A: Three. The quarterback to screw it in, and a couple of linemen to keep the Dallas players from getting the bulb.

Q: How many Jets players does it take to change a light bulb?

A: One, plus 60,000 fans to tell him what he's doing wrong.

The center hated quarterback Tim Nebraska's guts: the QB got the credit, while he took all the hits.

After a hard-fought victory, the center was interviewed by the press.

"What do you think of Tim's performance today?"

Not wanting to start a feud by saying anything detrimental, the center smiled.

"What can I say, except that I've got to hand it to him."

Q: What do Notre Dame coaches write on their players' uniforms?
A: Helmet, jersey, shoulder pads, shoes . . .

The little boy said, "Ma . . . do you love me?"
"Why of course I do!" she replied.
"Wouldja do anything for me?"
"Absolutely."
The boy said, "Then *please* divorce Pop and marry a Raider so I can go to the playoffs."

"Me caught de footbawl," said Bart, the college athlete, struggling through a class in grammar.
"No, no," said the professor, "*I* caught the football."
The athlete scratched his head. "Dat musta happened when I was on de bench."

Later in class, the teacher said, "Bart, tell me how to correct this: 'Coach, he am a poor receiver.' "
Bart answered, "Drill the sucker."

The math teacher didn't have much better luck.
"Now Bart," he said, "if I lay a helmet here, another helmet next to it, and one more beside that, what would I have?"
Bart thought, then answered, "Some messy helmets."

After failing everything but football, Bart called his teachers together and said, "Listen, people— I don't want to alarm you, but my daddy called and said that if I don't start gettin' better grades, somebody's gonna get the shit kicked outta them."

Q: What do you call a football player born on April 1?
A: A foolback.

Then there was the old referee who was mean to the end . . . and the quarterback, and the wide receiver, and . . .

Q: What's the difference between Prince Charles and a long bomb?
A: One is heir to the throne. . . .

The quarterback liked his fellow players, but demanded that one of them be traded. The reason? The fellow was constantly cracking dirty jokes and arousing him. It was the first time in history that an athlete had come to his end's wit.

Then there was the group of senators who came up with a plan to cut down on welfare rolls. They proposed expanding the NFL to 500 teams.

The lineman was in bed with Mrs. Jones when Mr. Jones pulled into the driveway.

"Where's the back door?" the lineman asked.

"We don't have one."

"Where would you like it?" he enquired.

The woman on crutches was telling her neighbor, "This weekend, my husband did something that shows how much he loves me. The football game had just started, when I tripped carrying the laundry down the steps. Broke both my legs. Now, you know how much my husband loves football—"

"I do," said the woman.

"Well, he didn't even wait for the end of the game to call an ambulance. Just as soon as halftime started, he was up and dialing the number. . . ."

The wife of a different football fan said to her friend, "After twenty years of marriage, our sex life is like the Super Bowl."

"You mean the noise, the excitement, the fun—"

"No," she said. "I mean it happens just once a year."

Q: What do you get when you cross an Oiler with an octopus?

A: A player that'll *still* fumble.

Actually, the Oilers don't fumble all the time. Only when they have the ball.

The naive football player finally worked up the courage to ask one of the cheerleaders for a date.

"I'm sorry," she said sweetly, "but I can't go out with you. I'm a lesbian."

The player asked, "What's a lesbian?"

"Well," said the woman, pointing to another cheerleader, "do you see Marcy over there? I'd like to get her alone, take off her outfit, and make passionate love to her."

The player walked back to the bench.

"How'd you make out?" asked a teammate.

"Not very well, but I did learn one thing about myself."

"What's that?"

The player replied, "I'm a lesbian."

Sitting at the Super Bowl, one Pole said to another, "Y'know, if it weren't so crowded here, a lot more people would come."

Horner chronically overslept and was always late for training, so the coach gave him an ultimatum: Show up on time or be cut from the squad.

That night Horner went to sleep early, and as the first light of dawn streamed through the window, he leaped from bed, drove to the field, and was the first player there.

"I did it!" he shouted. "I *did* it!"

"Yes," said the coach, "but where were you yesterday?"

Wilson sat beside a teammate. "Did you hear what the cheerleader said to the coach?"

"No."

"Then you *did* hear. . . ."

On their wedding night, rather prudish Franklin was alarmed when his new bride seemed right at home with sexual intercourse.

"Zelda," he said, "I—I hate to ask, but have you done this before?"

She blushed. "Once, my love."

That didn't seem so bad and he said, "Do you mind if I ask with whom?"

She replied, "The Indianapolis Colts."

Q: How did the veteran Phoenix quarterback manage to become Pope?

A: Why not? He'd been a Cardinal long enough.

The playboy college quarterback was under enormous pressure to win the game, pressure that wasn't helped by the coach's edict that the team stay away from women for a full week before the game.

After being celibate for a day, the player couldn't stand it any longer and masturbated. Unfortunately, the coach caught him.

"Jerk! I told you to show me some *discipline!* Save it until *after* the game!"

The quarterback nodded, and two days later, the coach stopped by his room to see how he was doing.

"Just great!" he said, whipping a jar out from under the bed. "So far I've saved three ounces!"

At another school, the coach was far more sympathetic. When one of his players became dizzy and ineffective due to sexual yearning, he hired a hooker. Luckily, she got the weak end off.

Hoping to spur attendance at home games, the Dallas front office commissioned the famed Polish designer Frederic Tepes to create new uniforms for the team.

To their unbridled horror, the new uniforms were transparent.

"How the hell do you expect our players to wear those?" screamed the general manager. "You can see right through the damn things!"

The snooty designer replied, "Not when the players are wearing them!"

Then there was the Polish player who brought iodine to training camp, just in case the coach cut him . . .

. . . and the field-goal expert who played football because he got a kick out of it. . . .

Q: Why did the coach buy wheelbarrows for the linemen?
A: He decided it was time they learned to walk on their hind legs.

Running backs Carlton and Carter had been drinking all night and finally snuck off to the lavatory to relieve themselves.

When they were gone, a customer walked over to the bartender.

"Say, aren't they Carlton and Carter of the Rams?"

"They are," said the bartender.

The man placed a ten-dollar bill on the table. "Take it all outta here," he said. "Give me a scotch, and see what the backs in the boys' room are having."

Q: What's written on the Christmas card sent out by the coach at Notre Dame?
A: Irish you a Merry Christmas.

Q: Why does the football season seem so long?
A: Because it goes in one year and out the other.

Then there was the fan who watched so much football on TV that his end zone grew. . . .

Q: What's the difference between someone with bad hair and an owner who loses free agents?
A: None. They both suffer from split ends.

Q: How did the quarterback become a hunchback?
A: He just played his intuition.

Down 28-3 in the third quarter, the coach called the quarterback to the sidelines.

"Hank," he said, "you've really got to take to the air more—"

"I would," screamed the quarterback, "if I was given some protection out there! Christ, I was tackled a half-dozen times in the first half!"

Growing irate, the coach roared, "That's all you ever talk about! Sacks! Sacks! Sacks!"

Q: How many Miami Dolphins does it take to screw in a light bulb?
A: Two. The other one recovers the fumble.

Then there was the college football star who got his varsity letter and had to have his girlfriend read it to him. . . .

Q: What's the difference between a fan at a Jets game and a customer at a bakery?
A: Big Apple turnovers make one of them sick.

A football coach is a man whose job is to predict what will happen on Sunday ... then explain, on Monday, why it didn't.

Q: What do an atheist and a losing football team have in common?
A: Neither of them has a prayer on Sundays.

The disgruntled Dallas fan was sitting in a bar after the Cowboys had lost yet another game.

"Those Cowboys are all a bunch of horses' asses!" he said to the bartender.

Hearing this, a strapping young cowboy ambled over. "Listen, bud. 'Round these parts, those're fightin' words."

"Sorry," said the other. "I didn't realize this was Cowboys country."

"It ain't. It's horse country."

"What position did you play in college?" the boy asked his uncle.

"I was a back."

"Full back or halfback?"

The man replied, "Drawback."

Then there was the coach who was made to order . . .

. . . and the man who made news when he was on his way to Veterans Stadium for a playoff game: he was hit dead-on by a train, bounced in front of a bus, and lived. The Eagles immediately signed him to play center against the 49ers. . . .

It turns out that there's a new ailment circulating among gridiron fans: football elbow. It comes from watching too much football while leaning on a bar.

Q: What's the difference between eggs and quarterbacks?

A: Scrambling eggs makes 'em go down easy, while scrambling quarterbacks won't.

Q: Which quarterback held his team together better than anyone in history?
A: Ken Stapler.

Q: Why do Tampa Bay fans die young?
A: They want to.

The man worked two jobs in order to send his son to Notre Dame so the young man could play football. After spending tens of thousands of dollars, what did the man end up with?

He got a quarterback.

A 49ers fan walked into a bar and told the bartender, "I'd like a San Franciscan drink."

The bartender gave him a puzzled look. "How do you make a San Franciscan drink?"

"Simple," said the man. "Just say, 'Montana's out for the rest of the season.'"

Before going to their respective stands, two hot-dog vendors were in the lavatory.

After relieving himself, one of the men went to leave.

"A responsible vendor remembers to wash his hands before he goes to work," the other called after him.

To which his colleague replied, "A responsible vendor learns not to piss on himself."

Q: Where to most of the Rams find their dates?
A: Ewe SC.

Two Poles were walking past Hofstra, where the Jets were in training. As they watched them doing push-ups, one Pole said to the other, "Do you think we should tell them that their girlfriends slipped away?"

After getting creamed, the quarterback was carried to the sidelines, where the team doctor was waiting.

The physician examined the player, then said, "I've got good news and bad news. The bad news is your knee is shot. You'll need surgery and will be out for the rest of the season."

The quarterback moaned. "What's the good news, then?"

The doctor smiled. "You know Jessica, the cheerleader? She's agreed to go out with me Saturday night."

The college gridiron star was taking an oral history exam.

The professor asked, "During the Revolution, the British were known as the redcoats. What do we call Washington's men?"

The football player answered without hesitation, "The Redskins."

Q: What does AT&T have in common with the Detroit team?

A: There's no joy when the Lions are down.

The football fan bumped into the Patriots quarterback on the street.

"Did anyone ever tell you how *good* you are—"

"Why thank you!"

"—and mean it?"

Then there was the college cheerleader who graduated magna cum loudest ...

... the free agent whose abilities left nothing to be desired, by anyone ...

... the Pole who was looking for kicks, so he laced up his mouth and went to Soldier Field ...

... the wide receiver who stumbled out of bounds, landed atop a cheerleader, and was penalized for illegal use of hands ...

... the Columbia University football coach who, after losing a record number of games, said that his boys were trying ... very trying ...

... and the playboy quarterback who had ten wives, three of them his own. ...

In fact, when the quarterback said he had a seven-figure income, he was talking about the number of women he was supporting.

And let's not overlook the latest rage: football solitaire. You take the field against the Falcons. ...

In fairness to the Falcons, one could say that they're the cream of their profession: they're always getting whipped.

Q: What's the difference between a priest and a lineman?
A: One prays on Sunday, the other preys on Sunday.

Sad but true: A Louisiana college suffered a budget cut in the sports department, meaning that their football team, the Wolves, had to buy inferior uniforms. These tore during every game, causing one rival to label them as "Wolves in cheap clothing. ..."

Aaron stood on line for Super Bowl tickets. He didn't exactly get great seats. In fact, the seats were so far—

—that the game was just a rumor.

—he was the only one in his row without a harp.

—he turned to the guy next to him and asked, "How do you like the game?"

The man answered, "Game, shmame. I'm on my final approach to Miami International."

The college junior and his date were at the big game when the quarterback was replaced by an up-and-coming star.

"Before the season's out, that player's going to be our best man," said the junior.

The young woman blushed. "Isn't this rather sudden?"

After another losing season, the college coach was asked by the press why he kept the godawful quarterback Sid Chu on the team.

"It's simple," he said. "The school gets a lot of money from the Asians, and I've got to use Sid to keep them happy."

The moral, he said, was that when the player graduated, he'd never again get stuck with a No Win Sid Chu, Asian.

"Son," said the college advisor to a student, "if you've got half a mind to play football, go right ahead. That's all it takes."

It's not that football players are dumb, but there once was a tackle who tripped down a flight of stairs, got up, looked around, and barked, "Hey! Who made all that noise?"

A football player walked into a bar carrying the team mascot, an armadillo, under his arm.

"Hey," said the bartender, "what're you doing with that pig?"

"That ain't no pig," said the player. "That's an armadillo."

"I know," said the bartender. "That's who I was talking to."

Then there was the sociable tackle: he loved his work because of all the people he ran into. . . .

The hulking fellow lumbered into the New York Jets office and asked to try out for the team.

The man looked mean, and the coach was impressed with his size. He was even more impressed when the fellow said he'd just spent four years playing for Yale.

"And what'd you say your name was?" asked the coach.

The man replied, "Yohnson."

GOLF

After a day of golf, Orlito walked into the house. Instead of kissing his wife as he always did, he simply fell into a chair.

His wife hurried over. "Honey, what's wrong? You look exhausted!"

"It was a terrible day," he said. "After we teed off, Leon had a heart attack, keeled over, and died!"

"Oh, that *is* terrible!" his wife said.

"And it got worse!"

"How could it be worse?"

"Because for the rest of the day, it was shoot, drag Leon, shoot, drag Leon. . . ."

After a rich invitational, golf star Ben Hurt and his rival Eli Sid were dressing in the locker room.

The two were chatting about the game, talking about the inconvenience of being on the road so many days a year, when suddenly Ben slipped on a pair of lady's underwear.

Eli stared.

"Ben! Since when have you been wearing *panties*?"

Ben frowned. "Since I came home from a tournament and my wife found them in the backseat."

Fresh from the Ozarks, hillbilly Jake went to the affluent suburbs of Missouri to try to earn some money. The first place he stopped was a country club. As he headed toward the front door, a man called to him from his car.

"Hey, son! Are you here to caddy?"

"Caddy, sir?"

"You know—carry my clubs for money."

"Yes, sir!" Jake grinned, and hurried over to the car.

While the man unlocked the trunk, Jake admired the sleek automobile.

"Here they are," the man said, pointing to the bag.

As Jake lifted it from the car, his eyes still on the vehicle, several tees fell from the side pocket.

"What are those?" Jake asked as he quickly scooped them up.

"They're tees. When you drive, you put your balls on them."

"Wow," gushed Jake. "Those Jaguar people think of everything, don't they?"

A short while later, all dressed and ready to play, the man teed up at the first hole. However, before he could even select a club, a young woman in a bride's dress came running across the course.

"You bastard!" she screamed. "You stinking, no-good bastard!"

"Aw, come on, hon," the man said, sighing. "Didn't I tell you, only if it *rains*?"

Not surprisingly, the golfer's fiancée ran off. Nursing spring water later in the clubhouse, he forgot all about the woman when a lovely young lady sat down beside him and struck up a conversation. Before long, he asked her to come back to his apartment with him.

"I'd love to," she cooed, "but there's something I have to tell you. I'm a hooker."

"No problem." The man smiled. "After a few hours in the hay, I'll show you how to hold the clubs differently."

Then there was another golfer whose wife dumped him after she learned that he'd been making five-footers on the green.

Sally Green was a terrific golfer and a great sport, but she got a terrible reputation after winning the championships at every country club in the county. Maybe it had something to do with the newspaper headline that announced her feat:
SALLY GREEN IS INTERCOURSE CHAMP!

Q: What's the difference between a man who makes love like a painter and one who makes love like a golfer?

A: The painter strokes for hours, while the golfer wants to get into the hole in as few strokes as possible.

It came to pass that the Church of England and the pope in Rome decided to heal the rift between their two houses. They opted to decide who would give in on the major issues in a most unusual manner: a high-ranking member of each church would be selected to play in a game of golf. The loser would make all the major concessions.

Not wishing to lose, the pope contacted golf star Tom Watson, made him a cardinal, and sent him to England to play.

Smiling with expectation, he turned on the radio and listened to the game. Much to his chagrin, however, Cardinal Watson was soundly defeated by Archbishop of Canterbury Nicklaus.

Moses, Jesus, and an elderly gentleman were out on the golf course. Moses was the first to tee off, and he sent his ball flying into a lake. Muttering under his breath, he stalked over, raised his club, parted the waters, and hit the ball to the fairway.

Jesus teed off next, and like Moses before him, he sliced the ball right into the water. Huffing with disgust, he stalked out onto the middle of the lake, lowered his club into the water, and knocked the ball onto the fairway.

At last it was the old man's turn. He hit the ball, which also went arcing toward the water. However, as it was about to hit, a fish rose from the water and swatted the ball with its tail. The ball struck a pigeon in the head, bounced up and landed on a tree, and rolled down a branch where it was nabbed by a squirrel. With the ball held between his little paws, the furry creature ran down the tree and across the fairway, and deposited the ball in the hole.

Red with anger, Jesus turned and snarled, "Nice, Dad, but did you come here to play golf or to show off?"

On a trip to L.A., the midwestern businessman told his novice advertising executive that he really enjoyed swinging nightclubs whenever he was in Southern California. Without further ado, the young exec arranged for him to visit a golf course with lights.

On the other end of the spectrum, there was the very human, very nearsighted golfer who was continually driving his caddy's nuts.

Q: Why are most golfers such god-awful lovers?
A: They can't get used to the hole being in the center of the rough.

Oscar and Felix were sitting on a park bench during their lunch hour, telling each other about the dreams they'd had the night before.

"I dreamed I was on the golf course," said Oscar, "an absolutely beautiful course where there was plenty of sun, no wind, no wait, and every shot I took landed on the green."

Felix said, "I dreamed I was before a crackling fire with two stunning women, just having a ball."

Oscar looked at him. "You had two women in your dream and you didn't call me?"

"Of course I did," said Felix. "But when your wife answered, she said you were out golfing."

After winning his first big tournament, a handsome young golfer was approached by a foxy young woman in the clubhouse.

"Tell me," she whispered, "are you as good off the green as you are on it?"

Smiling, he took the woman's hand and led her to his hotel room, where they made frantic love. When the golfer rolled off, the woman pulled him to her.

"A champion doesn't give up like that," she said, and the golfer made love to her again.

When they were finished, he slipped off, but the woman still wouldn't let him go.

"A champion should never stop when he's winning," she said, and taking a deep breath, the golfer went back for another round. This time when it was over, the golfer fell asleep on top of her, too exhausted to move.

"A champion doesn't give in to exhaustion," the woman said, and tried to get him going yet again.

More angry than mortified, the golfer looked down at her and said, "Hey—just what is par for this hole, anyway?"

Then there was the golfer whose sex life was awful because of his pitifully short putts.

While he was strolling along the promenade behind the country club, Ralph was struck on the head with a golf ball. He staggered back, dazed, and leaned against the wall; his vision was just clearing as he heard a man yelling to him from the course.

"I'm sorry!"

"Sorry!" Ralph moaned as the man ran over. "Mister, I'm going to sue you for at least $5 million."

"Look, I know you're upset, but I *did* say fore."

"What?"

"I said *fore!*"

Ralph rubbed his head. "Fine. I'll take it."

Derek was playing golf with his brother Hilton, a priest. No sooner had he teed off than his ball landed in a sand trap.

"Shit, I'm way off!" Derek cried.

His brother shifted uncomfortably. "Please, Derek, I'd appreciate it if you didn't swear. The lord doesn't approve, and he may strike you dead."

"All right, I'll watch it," Derek said. However, on the very next shot, he sent the ball arcing into the rough.

"Shit, I'm way off!"

Hilton frowned. "Derek, you promised—"

Derek apologized again. On his third shot, though, he swung and didn't come anywhere near the ball.

"Shit, I'm way off!" he screamed again.

Just as his brother was about to stalk off, a lightning bolt split the sky, struck Hilton, and reduced him to a pile of ash.

And suddenly, a voice boomed from above, "Shit, I'm way off!"

Derek did indeed have some strange encounters on the course. A week later, he was playing with his pal Marc and sent his first shot flying into deep rough. Trudging after it while Marc teed off, he found himself amid a field of buttercups. Selecting an iron, he began thrashing away, looking for the ball.

"Stop that at *once!*"

"Huh?" Derek gasped, and turned. Behind him was an elderly woman in a flowing white robe. She was frowning. "Who are you?" Derek asked.

"I'm Mother Nature, and for your insensitivity

toward my buttercups, I herewith decree that whenever you eat butter, you will become terribly ill for a full day."

With that, the woman transformed herself into a fine mist and dissipated.

Stunned, Derek forgot about the ball and stumbled back to his partner. However, when he returned to where they'd teed off, Marc was nowhere to be found.

"Where are you?" Derek cried.

A voice came from several hundred yards away. "I'm over here, looking for my ball."

"Over where? I can't see you!"

"Ahead! In the pussy willows!"

Derek felt his throat tighten. "Jesus, Marc, whatever you do, *don't swing your club!*"

The intern could find no cause for the man's illness and went to talk to his supervisor, Dr. Cohen.

"Tension and vomiting," Dr. Cohen said, examining the man's chart. "This one's easy."

"Really?" said the intern.

"Yes, I've seen it many times. Find out if the patient plays golf. If he does, tell him to stop. If he doesn't, tell him to start."

It was their twentieth anniversary, and Mrs. Digby said to Mr. Digby, "Honey ... do you remember the day we were married?"

"I'll never forget it," he said. "I sank a forty-foot putt the day before."

Then there was the man who discovered an easy way to eliminate strokes. He used an eraser.

Jenson bumped into Ludwig on the course.

"Care to explain why you need two caddies?" Jenson asked.

Ludwig replied, "It's my wife's doing."

"Your wife?"

"Yeah. She feels I don't spend enough time with the kids."

The tyro golfer asked his seasoned friend, "When do I get to use the putter?"

His friend said, "Hopefully, sometime before sunset."

Cheating Chuck arrived at the club and asked the caddy, "How much are six, five, and four?"

"Ten," said the caddy.

Chuck said, "You'll do."

Cheap Chad arrived shortly after Cheating Chuck and said, "Caddy, how are you at finding lost balls?"

"Excellent, sir."

"Very well. Find one, and let's get going."

Then there was the elderly golfer who complained, "Now that I'm rich enough to afford to lose balls, I can't drive them far enough to lose them!"

The novice golfer complained to his more experienced wife, "You know, I've swung at the ball ten times, but I haven't hit it yet."

"Well," she said, "keep at it. It's beginning to look a little concerned."

"How have you been playing?" Becky asked her friend Judy.

"I've been averaging in the midseventies."

"Honestly?" Becky asked.

"Heck," said Judy, "what's that got to do with it?"

Then there was the obese player who complained that if he put the ball where he could see it, he couldn't hit it, and if he put it where he could hit it, he couldn't see it.

The distracted golfer complained to his caddy, "Why on *earth* do you keep looking at that watch?"

"Sir," said the caddy, "this isn't a watch. It's a compass."

Frank and Raymond went to the first tee, from which Raymond knocked a drive 450 yards along the fairway. The ball landed on the green, rolled ahead, circled the lip of the cup once, then dropped in.

Frank nodded. "Very good. After I take my own practice shot, we'll get under way."

Later in the game, Frank said, "God, Raymond—I'd move heaven and earth to play par on this course."

Standing back as Frank took his fourth shot in the rough, Raymond said, "I'd start on heaven if I were you. You've already moved enough earth."

The golfer was in a sand trap with the consistency of quicksand. Carefully studying the terrain and then selecting his club, he focused all his attention on the ball. With a strong but measured swing, he whacked it free.

"Aha!" he cried exultantly to his partner. "Even Trevino couldn't have done better!"

"That's true," said his partner. "But then, Trevino never would have been *in* that predicament."

After a frustrating afternoon, the golfer said to his caddy, "My friend, you've got to be the worst caddy in all of golf."

"I don't think so," said the youth.

"Why not?"

The caddy replied, "That'd *really* be a coincidence."

After five strokes, the golfer was still in the bunker. Mustering all his strength and skill, he managed one more stroke and finally got out: they carried him away on a stretcher.

Jason was visiting his brother in Connecticut, and they decided to play some golf.

After knocking balls into the sand, water, and rough on the first three holes, Jason turned to his sibling and said, "Man, this is just about the toughest course I've played in my life!"

"How do you know?" his brother said. "You haven't played on it yet."

Midway through the third hole, the golfer turned to his smartmouth caddy and said, "Son— I just want you to know that when we get back, I'm going to report you for being such a wiseacre!"

"That's fine with me," the boy said. "By the time we get back, I'll be old enough to get a real job."

Then there was the golfer who was playing his first-ever game when he suddenly looked up like a startled deer and dived into a nearby cart.

"Why'd you do that?" his caddy asked.

Cautiously peering around, the golfer said, "Didn't you hear that?"

"What?"

"The guy up ahead yelled, 'Ford!' "

"Hear about the ball thief?" one golfer asked another.

"No, do tell!"

"I wouldn't putt it past her."

Q: What do you call nine holes played by drunks?

A: Golf, bagged.

The player stepped from the rough where his partner was waiting. He filled in his card.

"Two strokes!" screamed the partner. "Dammit, I stood here watching—you took five strokes!"

The other man frowned. "Don't tell me you're going to count the three it took to kill the squirrel trying to steal my ball!"

Then there was the avid golfer who got the shakes when Christmas carolers came to his door singing, "Over the river and through the woods . . ."

Two drunks were peering over the country club's stone wall, watching golfers.

When one of them landed in a sand trap, one drunk said, "Hell, he'll never get outta that!"

But the golfer swung with poise and confidence, and the ball soared off.

The next golfer landed in the rough, and the drunk said, "Watch—*he'll* never get outta that!"

But the golfer dug in his heels, kept his eyes on the ball, and it soared free.

The next golfer sent his ball soaring onto the green and straight into the cup.

The drunk grinned. "Now *this* guy's really screwed!"

Duncan was carting down the course when he saw a man up to his waist, then his chest, in quicksand. He was shouting and gesturing madly.

"Just a moment!" Duncan yelled. "I'll save you!"

"No!" screamed the golfer as the quicksand reached his chin. "Hand me my wedge!"

Another the-elements-be-damned golfer was explaining to a friend that he even played golf in the snow.

"What do you do," said the friend, "paint your balls a darker color?"

"No," said the golfer. "I wear two pairs of undershorts."

"The jerks!" Hardy snarled as he stormed into the house.

"What's wrong, darling?" his wife asked.

"The club assessed me $1,000 for striking my partner!"

"Unsportsmanlike conduct?" she asked.

"No," he replied, "wrong iron."

Brendon bumped into the new member in the clubhouse.

"So," he said, "how'd you do on your first day out?"

"Pretty well," said the newcomer. "Got a fifty."

"Fifty!" Brendon cried. "God, that's great! You going to play tomorrow? I'd like to join you."

"I'll be here," the new member said. "I want to try the second hole."

After recovering from that, Brendon asked the newcomer, "Well . . . er . . . what do you think of the greens?"

The new member said, "I don't believe I've met them yet."

After returning from his first day at the club, the novice golfer was greeted by his wife.

"Did you win?" she asked naively.

"In a manner of speaking," he replied. "I hit the ball more than anyone else."

The man ran to the clubhouse phone and called his physician.

"My kid just swallowed a box of tees!" he cried. "What do I do?"

The doctor replied, "Practice your putting."

The cheapest man in the club walked up to the buffet table, muttering, "Piss and damnation, I lost a ball today."

"What happened?" asked another. "String break?"

As her husband hung up the phone after arranging a golf game, Mary asked, "Why don't you play with Wilson anymore?"

"Would you play with someone who shaves strokes off his scorecard, moves the ball closer whenever no one's looking, and talks when someone else is playing?"

"I should say not," Mary replied.

"Well," said her husband, "neither would Wilson."

Then there were the Siamese twins who wrote a book about their experiences on the links. The title? *Tee for Two.*

Rudolph was practicing his game in the backyard when, in typical Rudolph fashion, a ball went awry and flew toward the neighbor's house. A moment later, there was a sound of shattering glass.

"Hey!" the neighbor screamed. "What the hell did you do!"

Rudolph glanced over at the circular opening

in the bay window. "You ought to congratulate me."

"*Congratulate* you? For breaking a window?" Rudolph said, "No. For making a hole in one."

Then there was the wag who pointed out that golf spelled backward was flog. . . .

Golf is very much like life. You're constantly driving hard, only to end up in the hole.

A golfer is someone who talks about business on the golf course and golf in the office.

"It's not so tough meeting new people," said the golfer. "All you have to do is pick up the wrong ball. . . ."

Smedley walked up to the groundskeeper.

"Sorry, old sport, but I'm afraid . . . well, I had a little accident on the seventh hole."

"An accident, sir?"

"Yes, I . . . I moved my bowels."

"I see," said the groundskeeper. "Well, not to worry. It'll only take me a moment to clean it up."

"I'm afraid it'll take longer than a moment," Smedley continued. "You see, I followed through."

"It was the most amazing thing," said Fenwick. "There I was, about to play out of the rough on the tenth hole, when what should crawl between my legs but a rattlesnake."

"Dear lord," said Prescott. "What did you do?"

"You know the old tree there?"

"Indeed I do. The one where the lowest branch is twenty feet from the ground."

"Right," said Fenwick. "I leaped up there in terror."

"And you were able to grab the branch?" Prescott said, astonished.

"Not on the way up," admitted Fenwick. "On the way down."

Dinsdale went to visit his fiancée's family on Philadelphia's fashionable Main Line.

"Tell me a little about your family, Dinsdale," said his fiancée's father.

"Well, sir, there isn't much to say. They're just ordinary, hardworking folks."

"I see," said the man. "You know, young man, as far as I'm concerned, nothing is more important than breeding."

Dinsdale squeezed his fiancée's hand. "We like it too, sir, but we also like to get in a little golf now and then."

Horace couldn't begin his game because the man before him was kneeling and chanting at the tee.

After a few minutes of this, Horace tapped the man on the shoulder.

"Mind if I ask what the hell you're doing?" Horace asked.

"Certainly. I'm saying a prayer to keep lions from the course."

"Lions," said Horace. "This is New Jersey ... there *are* no lions here."

The man smiled. "See? It works!"

Q: How many golfers does it take to screw in a light bulb?

A: Depends whether it's the first hole or the nineteenth.

The southern gentleman tried to sneak in a few holes of golf before church, but got fouled up when he got a flat.

He tried fixing it, then decided to leave the car and run to church. As he arrived, he saw a man coming out.

"Is Mass out?" he asked.

"No," said the man, "but yer trousers is all covered with grease."

The ball rolled into the rough and came to a stop beside an anthill. A pair of ants came out to investigate.

The golfer arrived then, and after ducking a few swings, one ant said to the other, "No doubt about it! If we want to keep from being hit, we'd better get on the ball!"

The little girl was with her father on the golf course.

"Daddy," she said, "why don't you want the little ball to go into the hole?"

Q: What's the difference between a religious fanatic and an obese golfer?
A: One's a holy roller, the other a roly holer.

Then there was the dyslexic golfer who was disappointed when she bought a record that she though contained par music . . .

. . . and the man who opened a haven for vulgar golfers called Par for the Course. . . .

And let's not forget the Pole who refused to take up the sport because he thought golf balls was an ailment . . .

. . . or the woman who was convinced her golf cart was trying to give her advice when it went, "Putt, putt, putt . . ."

. . . or the golf fanatic who, whenever he was away from the golf course, had a fairway look in his eye . . .

. . . or the caddy who was prized by golfers because he was a compulsive tee totaler. . . .

Remember the man who preferred golf to marriage? Well, seeing his bride-to-be, he softened and went off to be wed. One might say he'd learned to put the heart before the course.

Q: What's the difference between an ailing golfer and one who plays every Sunday?
A: One plays weakly, the other weekly.

Arthur said to Izzie, "Did you hear about the golfer who lost 288 balls in one year?"
"No."
"It's too gross."

One golfer tapped another on the shoulder.
"Excuse me," said he, "but would you mind terribly if I played through? I've just been informed that my wife has been taken gravely ill."

After listening to a golfer boasting about his game, one caddy turned to another and remarked, "This is the game that turned the cows from the pasture and let in the bull."

Potter, a sailor, had been stranded on the remote South Pacific island for three years. One day, he saw a beautiful woman floating on a piece of driftwood. He waded out and helped her ashore, then dragged in her big shoulder bag.

"Thanks," she said. "My boyfriend's yacht went down, and I'm the only survivor."

She reached into the bag, popped an aspirin, then pulled out a comb and began brushing her hair. She noticed his gaze upon her.

"How long have you been here?" she asked.

"It's been three years since my boat went down."

"Wow," she said, "you *have* been deprived." She smiled. "Want to play around?"

His eyes widened and he looked at the bag. "Dear Lord! Don't tell me you've got a set of clubs in there too!"

It was Craig's first trip to Japan, and feeling lonely, he went to a bar. Though he didn't speak the language, he spotted a lovely young lady and the glances they exchanged said it all. Before long, they were back in Craig's hotel room, thrashing about on the bed in the dark. Soon they were naked.

Immediately after he began making love with the woman, Craig heard her moan, "Gojira!" A moment later, she moaned it again, and louder. *"Gojira!"*

Inspired by her cry of approval, he worked on her with even greater passion.

The following morning, Craig met his Japanese host, Mr. Tsuburaya, on the golf course. When they reached the green, Tsuburaya made an excellent putt, which dropped right into the cup.

Thinking to compliment his host in Japanese, Craig thought back to the night before. "Gojira," he said, applauding politely.

Tsuburaya shot him a look. "What do you mean, 'wrong hole'?"

Then there was the golfer who was so cool and tactful on the golf course, the club coined a new term just for him: savoir fairway.

On the other hand, there was the golfer who invented a new kind of music, which consisted of yelling at the ball and swearing at the ground. Its name? Trap music.

Teabury bumped into Mintz on the golf course.

"I say—what made you postpone your wedding day?"

"Well, I figured out that my silver anniversary

would fall on a Sunday, and I always play golf on Sunday."

Horowitz was boasting, "I played Palmer on this course a week ago, and there was only a one-number difference between our scores."

"Really?" said another club member.

"That's right," said Horowitz. "He had 70 and I had 170."

Q: What do you call an unattractive, 300-pound lady on the links?
A: A golf bag.

Q: What do you call that same woman when she gets ready to play?
A: A tee bag.

Q: What's the difference between a club's best player and a club's biggest liar?
A: One's the club pro, the other the club con.

Q: Why did the club name a drink Lilac Crazy in honor of one of its members?
A: Because each time he went to the nineteenth hole, that's exactly what he did.

Not that all golfers are liars. There was once one who was as honest as the day is long ... in the North Pole during the winter.

"I'd love to make this shot," the golfer said to his companion.

"Why?"

"See that woman up there on the clubhouse balcony? That's my mother-in-law."

His companion shook his head. "It's nearly three hundred yards. You'll *never* hit her from here."

Then there was the golf equipment manufacturer who recalled a series of clubs because they weren't up to par....

The old priest and his young friend went golfing and, as usual, the game went well for the clergyman.

"God must be on your side *again*," said his friend. "You sink every putt you take!"

"Look at it this way," said the priest. "One day you'll bury me, and you'll have won the most important game of all."

"Won, shmun!" said his friend. "You'll *still* be first in the hole!"

HOCKEY

Q: Why aren't lepers allowed to play ice hockey?

A: Because it's just one face-off after another.

In a postmortem press conference after their Stanley Cup defeat, angry Flyers coach LeClark refused to accept any of the blame for their loss. Instead, he pinned it all on a penalty unjustly called against his star player, Claude DeKaque, a penalty that resulted in the other team scoring the winning goal.

The following morning, one clever journalist summed it all up with the following headline:

LECLARK SAYS LOSS IS, "JUST THE ICING ON DEKAQUE."

Goalie Craig Ogan was traded, and not only wasn't he happy about that, he hated having to get a thorough medical examination.

"Look," the hockey player told the doctor,

"I'm in perfect shape. Just sign my damn form and let me go."

"No can do," the doctor said. "If a problem surfaces during the year, it's my butt."

Ogan snorted. "Wanna make a little bet? If you find something, I'll give you a season pass, center ice, front-row seats."

"And if I don't?"

"You send that gorgeous nurse of yours in here for a half hour."

"You've got a deal," the medic said, and proceeded to give Ogan the most complete physical of either man's life.

When he was nearly finished, the doctor began to grow concerned. There was nothing wrong with Ogan, and he knew that his nurse would quit if she even learned what he'd agreed to.

As he pulled on a rubber glove and conducted a rectal examination, his mind raced furiously.

After a moment, he withdrew his finger.

"So," crowed Ogan, "it's like I said—nothing wrong, right?"

"Not so fast," the doctor said. Holding a tongue depresser in his left hand, he had Ogan open his mouth, pressed down on his tongue ... then slipped his gloved, feces-smudged index finger down the goalie's throat. It didn't take a second for Ogan to grow pale and throw up everything he'd eaten for the last month.

"Just as I thought," the doctor said triumphantly. "Stomach trouble."

The university research lab placed an order for twenty cages seven feet tall and five feet wide and deep. Since the lab usually ordered cages seven inches by five inches, the scientific supplier called the lab.

"I'm sure it was an oversight," the supplier said, "but you wrote feet instead of inches on your order."

"No," said the head scientist, "feet is correct. We've started using hockey players in our experiments."

"Hockey players?" the supplier gasped. "For God's sake *why?"*

The scientist replied, "We got too attached to the rats."

The same lab posted a rather unusual notice on the university bulletin board: "$500 for agreeing to partake in an unusual sexual experiment."

The line of volunteers was long until they learned that the experiment consisted of making love to a sexually frustrated she-wolf. All but one of the men left.

"Name?" the scientist asked the remaining volunteer.

"Gish."

"Major?"

"Hockey." The young man seemed embarrassed. "Excuse me, but there's one thing I need to know."

"What's that?"

"I'm a little short of cash. Would it be okay if I paid you off fifty bucks a week?"

Newlyweds Norman and Caryn were happy as could be until tragedy struck: while Norman was carrying his bride across the threshold, he stumbled and hit his head on a marble end table.

The young man was rushed to the hospital, where doctors gave Caryn the bad news.

"He'll live, but only five percent of his brain will ever be functional."

Caryn began to sob, and after a few minutes she pulled herself together and went to see her husband. To her surprise, he wasn't in his room, or anywhere else in the hospital. A police search failed to turn him up until weeks later, when Caryn received a call from Detective Vinnie Papa.

"We've found him, and he's fine!" Papa declared.

"Where?" the joyous woman demanded.

"He's coaching hockey in Philadelphia."

The rookie star settled in for a pregame interview, his first.

"You're from Minnesota," said the sportscaster. "What part?"

The player replied, "All of me, sir."

After a game, the hockey player went to the pizza place and ordered a pie.

The waiter asked, "Would you like that cut into six or eight pieces, sir?"

"Eight," said the athlete. "I'm really hungry."

Q: What do you call a hockey player who turns down a beer?

A: Dead.

The sixteen-year-old girl brazenly entered the hockey-team locker room and ran up to her lover.

"We've got to talk, Jean-Claude," she said.

"Not now," he replied. "I'll be in big trouble if I miss this period."

"You're *in* big trouble!" she shot back. "I missed mine."

Then there was the Polish hockey team that drowned during spring training. . . .

Edmonton's Wayne LeRoque was told that the Sports Bar in Chicago was a popular gathering place for athletes. Thus, when his team was in town, he made sure to stop by. It was early in the night and the place wasn't very crowded, so he struck up a conversation with a man seated at the bar.

After a few minutes, LeRoque realized that the guy was a mobster, not an athlete.

"So you play basketball, eh?" the gangster said.

"Hockey."

"Hockey, basketball . . . what's the difference? Me? Golf's my game. I got a 280 today."

"Gee, that's great," said LeRoque, stifling a laugh.

"Great, shmate. I like to bet on games, 'at's all. You bet on your baseball games?"

"Hockey."

"Hockey, baseball ... what's the difference?"

"No, I'm afraid I don't bet on hockey," LeRoque said, but his mind was working. He himself swung a mean iron, and could beat a 280 with his eyes closed. He saw a chance to make some bucks.

"Tell you what," said LeRoque. "I've got time tomorrow morning. What do you say we play some golf with a little side bet?"

"I never bet little," said the gangster. "A half mil's my speed."

LeRoque didn't have that kind of money, but with a 280 handicap there was no way this man was going to beat him.

"What'd you get the game before 280?" LeRoque asked, just to be sure.

"I got a 290. An' before that, a 270."

Smiling, LeRoque agreed to the game. The mobster said he'd bring the equipment and pick LeRoque up in the morning.

The next day, a magnificent limo pulled up and the hockey player got in. As he settled down between the mobster and one of his gun-toting goons, he saw not golf bags, but a pair of bowling bags resting at his feet.

"Hey," LeRoque said nervously, "what're these for?"

"Our game."

"But you said we were playing golf!"
"Golf, bowling . . . what's the difference?"

Q: Why does the ice start to melt after a hockey game?
A: Because all the fans go home.

Q: Why don't the Chicago Black Hawks and St. Louis Blues ever brawl?
A: Because they're already black and blue when they get on the ice.

The Yale player was penalized for icing and grew irate, and was promptly ejected for using improper language. In his rage, he'd split an infinitive.

Father O'Connor was torn between hearing confession and watching the Stanley Cup playoffs. Opting to do his spiritual duty, he nonetheless took a radio and earplug into the booth with him.

After confessing, Paul joined his friend Sal.

"How'd it go?" Sal asked.

"Okay, I guess."

"You guess?"

"Yeah," said Paul. "I told him about how I cheated on my exam, and he made me sit in the booth for two minutes."

It was the first time in centuries that the Whalers made the playoffs, and the Hartford fans lined up for tickets the day before they went on sale.

Shortly before the box office was due to open, a short, stocky man walked along the line and stepped in front of an ox of a guy in front.

"Hey," said the brute, grabbing the man tightly around the neck and pitching him aside, "what the hell ya think yer doin'?"

Rubbing his throat and picking himself up, the small fellow once again stepped in front of the giant. And once again, the big man clutched him around the neck and threw him a good two yards.

Struggling to his feet once again, the little man cleared his throat and said, "Listen, asshole—you do that again and I'm not going to open the door!"

Sad to say, hockey fans are actually brighter than most hockey players.

After defecting from Poland, the Olympic hockey star went to try out for the Maple Leafs. The coach watched, amazed, as he skated around every defender, checked with aplomb, and barely missed a shot he took on the goal.

After the tryouts, the coach took the player aside.

"You did great," he said, "but how are you at passing the puck?"

"Great," said the Pole, and picking one up, he

swallowed it in one big gulp. "You'll have it back first thing in the morning."

The general manager of the New York Islanders walked up to the coach.

"I've got good news and bad news," he said. "The good news is that God himself just called to wish us good luck in the playoffs against the Flyers."

"That's terrific!" the coach beamed. "What's the bad news?"

"He called from Philly."

The playboy hockey star was sent to the hospital with a concussion.

After looking in on him, one nurse was stopped by another.

"Is he making progress?" she asked.

"He's trying," said the other, "but I prefer a man who has all his teeth."

"I hear the Bruins just had a no-hitter," the young lady said to her boyfriend.

"The Bruins? You sure you don't mean the Red Sox?"

"No, the Bruins," she insisted. "They played an entire game without throwing a single punch."

Q: What's the difference between a hockey player and an Italian housewife?
A: Nail polish.

Q: What's another difference between a hockey player and an Italian housewife?
A: After the third period, the hockey player showers.

Q: What's a seven-course meal to a Maple Leaf?
A: Back bacon and a six-pack.

Q: What's the difference between playing for the Bruins and playing for the Islanders?
A: In Boston, they enjoy beans. On Long Island, they only have the Sound.

The night before a playoff game, two hockey stars snuck out of the hotel for a few drinks. Before long, they were hopelessly inebriated.

"Say," said one, "what time is it?"

"Dunno," said the other. "Ain't nine yet, though."

"Why d'you say that?"

" 'Cause curfew is nine, and we ain't back yet."

The following morning, when the two players showed up for practice, the coach asked, "Did either of you miss curfew?"

One looked at the other and said, "I wouldn't miss it, would you?"

Then there was the hockey star who was offered $1.5 million to write his autobiography. Six months later, he handed in the story of his BMW.

Q: What's the difference between an actor in a hit show and a hockey player?
A: One sticks with a play....

Q: What do you get when you cross a Canadian with a groundhog?
A: Six more weeks of hockey.

The physician and hockey coach were debating the merits of their respective professions.

"Coaches teach young men to be aggressive, confident winners," said the coach.

"Exactly my point," replied the doctor. "You're hardly turning them into angels."

The coach shot back, "No—I guess you doctors have us beat there."

After leaving hockey, superstar Gordie Howe decided to become a lawyer. Upon passing his exams, he was courted by many firms, but signed with the one that put his name on the door: Dewey, Lye, and Howe.

Since baseball was such a hit, the Japanese entrepreneur decided to import ice hockey. Unfortunately for him, no one had a yen for it.

To stay loose before the big game, the Montreal hockey team went to a comedy club in Detroit. A ventriloquist came on, and his act consisted mainly of poking fun at the intellectual capacity of Canadians.

Before the fellow was halfway through his act, one of the hockey players bolted from his seat.

"Listen, you!" he shouted. "I don't want to hear another crack about how dumb Canadians are—"

"Sorry," said the ventriloquist, "but they're just jokes—"

"Shut up!" raged the hockey player. "I'm not talking to you, I'm talking to that squirt on your knee!"

Then there was the hockey player who finally learned to count to twenty-one, and was arrested for indecent exposure . . .

... and the even dumber one who took a woman on a date, and when she rubbed his thigh and asked to see his organ, he drove her to the arena and showed her the Wurlitzer. . . .

Nor should we forget the Polish hockey fan who asked for a ticket to just the first two periods, since he was a little short of cash.

After winning the NHL championship, the team invited sportswriters, stadium personnel, and others to a hotel suite for a big bash.

Two fans also snuck in, and got incredibly drunk. The next morning, when they woke up, they found themselves in an alley.

"Boy," said one, "that was a helluva party."

"Sure was," said the other. "I just wish we'd been able to thank our hosts."

"Do you remember what room they were in?"

"No. All I remember is that the suite was on the twentieth floor, and it had a silver toilet."

The other rose. "Come on. That shouldn't be too tough to find."

Heading back to the hotel, they went up to the twentieth floor and began knocking on doors.

"Is there a silver toilet here?" they asked at the first suite.

The door was slammed in their faces.

"Is there a silver toilet here?" they asked at the next suite.

Again, the answer was a slammed door.

"Is there a silver toilet here?" they asked at the suite.

The man who answered the door frowned. "Hey, Guy!" he shouted over his shoulder. "Here's the asshole that shit in the Stanley Cup."

The hockey star was playing away, so he stopped in the drugstore for supplies.

"I'd like some deodorant," he said.

"Certainly, sir. Stick or spray."

"Stick."

"The ball kind?"

"No," said the player, "the underarm kind."

Q: What do they call it when the Toronto team plays in Chicago without its top star?

A: Away, without Leaf.

Then there was the Boston fan who snuck into the locker room to see what was Bruin....

One man turned to another at the Boston bar.

"Have you heard the joke about the Bruins?" he asked.

"Before you tell it," said the other, "I ought to warn you—I play for the Bruins."

"That's okay," said the man. "I'll tell it nice and slow."

"How'd it go?" the father asked his son as he returned from a hockey match.

"We got vitamins for the butt, Pop," said the boy.

"Excuse me?"

The boy said, "We got our asses B-10."

Q: What does a court of law have in common with a hockey rink?

A: What you find there is just ice. . . .

Then there was the skater who was cut from the Sabres. He bled all over the ice. . . .

Another much-battered skater complained at a press conference, "Ya know, I ain't as dumb as I look."

A reporter shouted back, "No one *could* be!"

To prove he wasn't the idiot everyone had always claimed he was, the retiring hockey player held a press conference and agreed to answer any and all questions.

"What's your name?" a reporter joked.

The player began counting on his fingers, and after he'd ticked off eleven, he said, "Guy."

The reporter said, "But Guy's only three letters."

"Hah!" said the player. "Dat shows what *you*

know." Holding up his hand, he ticked off his fingers as he said, "Happy birthday to you, happy birthday to you, happy birthday dear . . ."

Truth is, Max was pretty forthcoming about his modest intellectual gifts. As he told the press conference, now that he'd made his mark, he intended to learn to write his name.

Q: What's a gay Canadian?
A: Someone who'd rather go out with girls than play hockey.

Q: Why do hockey players eat beans before a game?
A: So they can take a Jacuzzi after the game.

HORSE RACING

Q: What's the definition of a racetrack?
A: A place where windows clean people.

Q: What's the definition of a racehorse?
A: An animal that can take several thousand people for a ride at the same time.

Mort and Bernie went to the track, and while they were there, Mort had a heart attack and dropped dead.

Wanting to break the news gently to Mort's wife, Bernie stopped by the house and said, "Jackie, I've got some bad news for you. Your husband lost your entire savings at the track."

"That bastard!" she screamed. "I hope he drops dead!"

Bernie said, "Funny you should mention that. . . ."

Q: How can you tell when there's a Polish jockey at the track?
A: He's riding a donkey.

Q: How can you tell when there's a Scotsman at the track?

A: He bets two bits on the donkey.

Q: How can you tell when there's an Italian at the track?

A: The donkey wins.

Q: Why aren't there any groupies just for jockeys?

A: Because no woman likes a low blow.

Q: Why do Poles make bad jockeys?

A: Because they keep stopping to ask directions.

Roland owned the fastest young stallion in the county, but there was a problem. Whenever the horse ran in a race, he'd stop to wink at the mares. Unfortunately, there was only one solution, and so Roland had the horse gelded.

A few weeks later, the healed horse was back at the starting gate. Roland watched him carefully. There were mares everywhere, but the horse's eye didn't stray. Satisfied that the animal had only the track in mind, Roland was confident he'd made the correct decision.

Just then the gun sounded, the horses bolted from the gate—and suddenly, the horse stopped, turned, and walked timidly back to the gate.

Roland ran over. "What the hell is wrong with you, you four-legged moron? Why'd you stop like that?"

"I've still got my pride," the horse said. "I mean, how would you feel if you started from the gate and some jerk yelled into the loudspeaker, 'They're off'?"

After a day at the track, Edgar walked in the front door and was greeted by his wife.

"How did you do, hon?" she asked.

"Do? Let me tell you one of the most amazing things that ever happened. What's today's date?"

"June sixth."

"Correct. And the day?"

"Saturday."

"Sixth day of the week, sixth day of the sixth month. So, comes the sixth race, what do you think I did?"

"Bet on the sixth horse," his wife said, an expectant smile pulling at her mouth.

"Bingo! I bet everything we had on him. And guess what happened?"

"He won?"

Edgar replied, "No. He came in sixth."

Q: Why do racehorses hate being put out to pasture?

A: Because everywhere they turn, it's nag, nag, nag.

After losing a bundle, the young man stepped up to the bar at the track.

"Give me something tall, cold, and full of scotch," he said.

Hearing this, a wretched man sitting beside him said, "If you wait a few minutes, I'll go and fetch my wife."

The horse ran a helluva race, but still managed to lose by a nose. Afterward, to show his admiration for a noble effort, the jockey took the horse out for a drink.

The man and the animal drew stares as they walked into the bar. When they sat down, the horse turned and glared into the room.

"Hey," he said angrily, "don't look at me like that. I'm over twenty-one."

Q: What did they call the genetically engineered racehorse that could run 3.26 light-years a second?
A: Parsecretariat.

The racehorse owner put her Triple Crown winner together with a prize mare, but nothing happened. The next morning, she called the vet, who came right over.

After examining the Thoroughbred, the vet said, "There's nothing wrong with your horse, but I gave him a shot of vitamins. That should make him a little livelier in stall."

The next morning, the owner called the vet once again.

"Doc," she said, "nothing happened again last night."

"You were watching?"

"No—"

"Then how do you know?" the vet asked, slightly annoyed. "Did you expect to have a foal overnight?"

The owner said, "No, but I *did* expect to see some happy faces this morning!"

Eventually, the Triple Crown winner became a sire. Shortly thereafter, both he and his mate suffocated in a fire at the stable.

Heartbroken, the owner brought them to a taxidermist.

"You want them mounted?" he asked.

"No," the woman replied. "Standing side by side will be fine."

Little Trudy was determined to be the first woman to ride a horse to victory in the Triple Crown. To that end, each and every day, when she came home from school, she raced her beloved Appaloosa, Dotty, around the farm.

One afternoon, Trudy came home and was greeted by her mother. The woman was wearing a forlorn expression.

"I'm afraid I have some bad news," she told Trudy. "Dotty was killed today by a runaway tractor."

Trudy got teary-eyed, then just nodded and walked out toward the barn. When she got there, she screamed loud enough to be heard in the next state.

"Mama!" she wailed when her mother arrived. "Where's Dotty?"

"I told you, honey ... Dotty is dead!"

"Oh, God!" Trudy shrieked hysterically. "I thought you said *Daddy!*"

The bank president came in to check on the local branch before the fiscal year came to a close.

"Where's DiFate?" he asked, demanding to see the manager.

One of the tellers replied sheepishly, "He's at the track."

"At the track, in the middle of business hours?" he roared. "Whatever for?"

The teller said, "It's his last stab at balancing the books."

Every day, Mr. Epstein went to the track and bet in every race. He got to know the man at the window, Russ, quite well.

One day, Mr. Epstein came to the window and bet on four different horses in one race.

"That's a new one for you," said Russ. "You usually bet just one horse."

"I know, but it's got to do with my system."

"Which system is that?" asked Russ.

"Each morning, I stick a pin in the betting sheet to choose my horses."

"So what happened today?"

Mr. Epstein replied, "I lost my pin, so I had to use a fork."

Horse maniac Mr. Diggle was rushing to the racetrack when a state trooper pulled him over.

"What's the hurry?" asked the officer.

"My wife's having a baby," Diggle replied.

The trooper looked into the car. "Yeah? Then where is she?"

"At home," Diggle said. "And if I don't place my bet *fast*, I won't get back in time to take her to the hospital."

"So," Mrs. Miller asked her son, "how did you and Daddy like your day at the zoo?"

"It was lots of fun," said the boy. "Daddy even bought me ice cream to celebrate."

"Celebrate what?"

"When one of the animals won and paid him ten to one."

Then there was the farmer who crossed his bookie with a hen and got a chicken that laid odds. . . .

Jockey Bill Abram moonlighted as a songwriter and took quite a ribbing from his fellow riders.

"I've heard you sing your songs," said one, "and I think they stink."

"What would convince you I'm good?" asked the composer.

The other rider thought a moment. He looked around the stable. "Mister, you write a love song about horse shit, and I'll kiss your ass before the next race."

The next day, Abram came to the track with his guitar. As everyone was suiting up, he cornered his critic and sang, "She was a groomer who loved all the jockeys; you might say the horse manure."

Abram didn't bother putting on his trousers.

Alvin spent half his waking hours at the track. After losing a small fortune, he decided to go to Gamblers Anonymous. Alas, he went to a meeting of How to Gamble by mistake. Instead of coming out all better, he came out all-bettor.

Then there was the luckless guy who ran out of money and continued to bet the horses mentally. In no time flat, he lost his mind.

A famous southern announcer was calling a race at Belmont. Suddenly, a sedan plowed through the gate, skidded along the tracks, and crossed the finish line.

After observing the spectacle, the announcer remarked, "Ladies and gentlemen ... this is the first time I've ever witnessed a fo'-do' finish."

Ada Michaelson was called to serve on the jury, but begged off because she was opposed to the death penalty.

"I'd like you to hear something about the case," the prosecutor pressed, "because it does not involve murder. A woman earned $5,000 and gave it to her husband to pay the travel agent for a vacation in Hawaii. Instead of so doing, the man went to the track and lost every dime."

Ada said, "I'll serve—and please forget what I said about the death penalty."

The jockeys were having lunch.

"Yeah," said one, "as soon as I realized the race was crooked, I got out of it."

The other asked, "How much?"

Then there was the rather dim Secretariat fan who bought two souvenirs of the famous race-horse: a bronzed hoof from the adult horse, and another from when it was a colt.

Q: How can you tell that it's a Pole watching the races on TV?
A: He's using binoculars.

Q: What did one racehorse say to another?
A: I can't remember your mane, but your pace rings a bell.

Two days before the Kentucky Derby, the odds-on favorite took ill.

Frantic, his owners called the vet, who injected the horse with antibiotics.

Inside the horse, a pair of bacteria were hiding from the medicine. But the vein they were in was too small, and thinking the coast was clear, they moved to another vessel—where they were promptly slaughtered by waiting antibodies.

The moral: Don't change streams in the middle of a horse.

Then there was the ill-fated jockey who was nicknamed "Centaur," because he ran each course like a horse's ass.

Q: What does a championship racehorse have in common with Al Capone?
A: One runs in the Preakness, the other runs from that prick, Ness.

Milton bumped into Stan at the racetrack.

"Stan, you look miserable. Lose again?"

Stan wailed, "I came here with enough dough to choke a horse and I made a terrible, terrible mistake."

"What's that?"

Stan replied, "I bet on him instead."

On the way out, Stan saw a priest blessing the horse.

"Father, I wouldn't waste my time blessing that horse," said Stan. "He's a loser ... I just blew a bundle on him."

"So did I," said the priest. "I'm reciting last rites."

As Stan summed up his escapades to a friend, "The track—for my money, you can't beat it."

The jockey walked into the doctor's office.

"Doc," he said, "I just don't understand it. Every time it rains, I get dressed and walk to the track—and my balls hurt."

After examining the patient, the doctor grabbed a pair of scissors, made a few snips, and sent the little man on his way.

A few days later, the jockey called.

"Doc, I just wanted to thank you for helping me. Two days it's rained, and my balls haven't hurt at all. I've been meaning to ask you—what exactly did you do?"

"Simple," the physician replied. "I cut three inches off the tops of your galoshes."

Having lost all but his last dollar at the track, Val walked up to a stranger and said, "Give me a hundred-to-one odds, and I'll pose a simple question you can't answer."

Being a gambling sort, the stranger agreed.

"Which has more legs," Val asked, "one horse or no horse?"

"One horse," answered the man.

"Wrong," Val replied as he snatched the C-note. "No horse has five legs."

With the hundred bucks in hand, Val found another dupe. He bet the sap that the first ten horses they saw would have only two dozen hooves between them.

The two walked to the stables, where Val promptly counted off twenty fore-feet. . . .

The owner of the thoroughbred Rosinante approached the groom, who happened to be Polish.

"The Preakness is in four days," said the owner, "and Rosinante here has been running a little slow. We have to make the horse fast. Any suggestions?"

"Not to worry," said the groom. "I'll take care of it."

Three days later, word reached the owner that the horse had died. Storming over to the stables, he grabbed the groom by the throat.

"How did Rosinante die? What the hell did you *do*?"

"I did just what you said," gurgled the groom.

"What *I* said?"

"Yes, sir! You wanted to make him fast, so I stopped feeding him!"

However, the Pole did get one thing right when he told another groom that horses eat best when there isn't a bit in their mouths....

The man came home from the racetrack.

"Sorry, hon," he said to his rather ditzy wife. "I lost all six races."

"That's all right." She smiled. "I don't think I could have made it around the track even once."

Then there was the man who went to the track hoping to meet Lady Luck, but wound up becoming intimate with Miss Fortune.

Indeed, racetracks happen to be very intimate places. Most people who go there get to kiss their money good-bye.

In other words, "hot tips" are only good for people who have money to burn.

It was the most remarkable race ever run. The horse was a hundred-to-one shot, yet he pulled ahead of the pack.

Then, just a few yards from the finish line, the animal glanced back and tragedy struck. He saw a horse's face for the first time and dropped dead from the shock.

Then there was the horse who was named Aristocrat, because he was the last in his race....

Rodney was a die-hard baseball fan, but one day a friend convinced him to go to the track. The two placed their bets on a long shot, Applegarth Whitney, then went to the grandstand to watch.

The race was a close one between Applegarth and the favorite, C.B., and watching the two race neck and neck in the stretch, Rodney couldn't take the tension any longer. Leaping to his feet, he cupped his hands to his mouth and shouted, "Slide, dammit! *Slide!*"

Q: What's the difference between horse races and queens?
A: None. Both are the sport of kings.

Hector shuffled into the bedroom.

"Something terrible happened on the way to the racetrack," he told his wife. "I made it."

"Seriously," said Hector, "I *did* bet on a good horse. I mean, it took nine horses to beat him!"

Q: How can you tell when a jockey isn't terribly confident of victory?
A: He's carrying a book for the ride.

When all is said and done, a racetrack is the one place you can go and have a good time without having any fun.

JOGGING

"I'll tell you," Cindy said to Joan as they took their morning run, "that cheating husband of mine has made me so mad I can't keep a scrap of food down."

"Then why don't you leave him?" Joan asked.

"I will," Cindy replied, "just as soon as I get down to a hundred."

Lacking the stamina to climb stairs, mow the lawn, or do other chores around the house, Moe went to see his doctor.

After giving the man a thorough examination, the doctor said, "Moe, there's nothing wrong with you that some exercise wouldn't cure. I suggest jogging. Do a half mile a day, and let me know how you're making out by the end of the week."

At week's end, the doctor received a call from Moe.

"Good to hear from you," the physician said. "You sound great."

"I *feel* great," Moe said.

"How's that lawn look?"

"Beats me," Moe said. "I'm over three miles from home."

Q: What's the difference between a woman jogging and a sewing machine?
A: A sewing machine has just one bobbin.

Jennie was an experienced jogger, and she urged her out-of-shape friend Patty to run along with her. As they started down the pleasant suburban street, Jennie said, "The most important thing to remember is that a pit bull lives in the house at the corner. He usually sits there quietly, but if he does run toward you, just throw something at him and hopefully he'll go away."

"What if there's nothing to throw?" Patty asked.

Jennie said, "Don't worry. If he charges, there will be."

The little kid paced the elderly jogger for a spell.

"How long've you been running?" asked the kid.

"Since I was sixteen."

"Wow," said the kid. "You must be tired!"

After jogging for a while, dumb Donald noticed that his wallet was missing. Realizing it must have fallen from his pocket when he stumbled in the park, he retraced his steps.

Remembering the lovely young lady who'd been reading not far from where he fell, he ran over to her.

"Pardon me, but did you notice if I lost my wallet a few minutes back?"

"Search me," she said.

He did, but the only wallet he found was hers.

While Kevin was out jogging along the beach in Malibu, he came upon an oil-covered duck. Gently carrying the bird home, he carefully cleaned and fed it, then set it free.

"Just a minute," the duck said.

"Y-you talk?"

"Of course," said the duck, "and I want to thank you for what you did. Come on—let me buy you a drink."

Never having met a talking duck, Kevin agreed, and the two walked to the local bar.

As they sat down at a table, Kevin ordered. So did the duck.

"Remember," the duck said to Kevin, "this is my treat."

The waitress overheard and grinned. "Excuse me, Mr. Duck, but *you're* paying?"

The duck nodded.

"How?"

He answered, "Just put it on my bill."

The novice jogger said to the experienced runner, "I've heard that you can protect yourself from dogs by carrying a rolled-up magazine while you run. Is that true?"

Said the other, "It all depends on how fast you carry it."

Q: What did the jogger do when she was run over by a steamroller?
A: Nothing. She just lay there with a long face.

After a dismal showing in the Boston Marathon, the reporter asked the former champion, "To what do you attribute your loss in today's race?"

The runner replied, "The agony of de feet."

Q: What's the difference between a commuter and a marathoner?
A: One runs for a train....

Q: What's the difference between a runner who strengthened his legs by jumping rope and one who didn't?
A: They both skipped it.

Then there was the Polish marathoner who filled his canteen with prune juice because he heard it would help him keep running and running . . .

. . . and the young lady who jogged barefoot so she could avoid a run in her stocking. . . .

Q: What's a wiener?
A: The person who comes in first in the Mexico City Marathon.

The Polish jogger wanted to look his absolute best for the New York marathon, so he told his wife to clean his running shoes then iron his socks.
Unfortunately, she burned his feet.

But did that stop the Pole? Absolutely not. As he painfully slipped on his footwear, he muttered, "The shoe must go on."

Q: What's the best way to describe an out-of-shape marathoner?
A: A sore loser.

Then there are the Scandinavian runners, who have a simple rule of thumb: If you've reached the last Lapp, you must be near the Finnish line.

One of those runners was nicknamed "Pants," not because of the way she breathed, but because of the way she always slacked off. . . .

Q: What do you call a herd of marathoners?
A: A pride of loins.

Q: What's the difference between someone who takes up jogging and a billionaire who adopts a baby boy?
A: One wants a little sun and air, the other a little son and heir.

One old-timer went for a walk with a friend.
"God," he said, "when I was a lad, I thought nothing about running ten miles a day."
"And now?" asked the friend.
"Now, I don't think so much of it."

"Did you hear about Aunt Charlotte?" Nan asked her brother. "She's not only walking in her sleep, she's jogging."
"That's awful. What does the doctor say?"

"He says to let her. That way, she can get her exercise and rest at the same time."

The two hillbilly kids met at school.
"Say, Jake," said one. "I hear you've taken up joggin'."
"Yeah, Hoke. It's good for the ass."
"The ass? How's it good for the ass?"
Jake replied, "Keeps buckshot out of it."

For her first run, obese Bertha showed up at Julie's house in a Day-Glo Spandex yellow jogging suit with blue and orange stripes.
Bertha noticed her friend's horrified gaze.
"I know it's ugly," Bertha said, "but I got it for an outrageous figure."
"I'll say," said Julie. "And what did it cost?"

"Jogging is an excellent way to kill germs in the circulatory system," the doctor told his Polish patient.
"Terrific!" said the patient. "How do we get them to start?"

Q: Most people who wear skintight jogging suits tend to accentuate what part of the body?
A: Their nerve.

MOUNTAIN CLIMBING

The Poles were determined to be the first ones from their country to climb Mount Everest. And they would have succeeded too, if they hadn't run out of scaffolding fifty feet from the summit.

Hans was telling a friend about his climbing trip in the Himalayas.

"There I was," he said, "nearly four miles up, when my supplies ran out. I staggered through the snow and wind until I came upon a village that consisted entirely of women. It took months, but they nursed me back to health."

"Not bad," said the friend.

"Ah, but there was a catch. It turns out that all the women there either had a venereal disease or tuberculosis."

"*That's* bad," the friend said. "So what did you do?"

"Used my head," said Hans. "If the woman coughed, I jumped her bones."

Then there was the mountaineer who made a fortune taking a billionaire oilman on climbs. He made quite a bundle until one day his business fell off. . . .

One climber said to the other, "Did you know they have a special mountaineering lingo in Colorado?"

"No kidding."

"Nope. They call it Pike-speak."

Q: What do you call a mathematician mountain climber who loses his grip?

A: The summer giving way to the fall.

The mountain-climbing instructor was a brilliant sportsman, but a lousy communicator.

After spending three days with a new student, he had been unable to teach her even the basis of mountaineering.

"I give up," he said. "Trying to teach you is useless. It's like knocking my head against the side of a mountain."

"That may be," said the irate student, "but since you brought it up, I can't think of anyone who could possibly do himself less harm."

Q: What did they call Sir Edmund Hillary after he spent a night atop Everest?

A: Cold.

Q: What do you call a broken mountaineering pick?
A: An anticlimb ax.

The three mountaineers were discussing life and death.

"Me?" said one. "I want to die trying to climb the western slope of K2 all alone."

Another said, "That's romantic. But I'd rather perish climbing Mount Saint Helens and having it erupt."

The third thought for a moment and said, "As for me, I want to be shot by a jealous husband."

The insurance salesperson went to the mountain-climbing club to peddle her wares. No one was interested.

"Listen," she said, calling on her ace in the hole, "I'm sure you all heard about Jones. Last week, he took out a policy with me—and a day later he broke both arms and legs in a fall."

"Sure," said one of the club members, "but Jones was one of the lucky ones!"

The problem with having mountaineers for friends is that they're rarely on the level. . . .

Q: How does a mountain climber file pitons?
A: Under *P*.

Q: Where did the climber go after the Sherpa guide led him up Annapurna instead of Everest?

A: Small-climbs court.

OLYMPICS

After years of taking drugs in private, the track star finally got caught. It was his fault, though. When the Olympics committee told him to come in for drug testing, he thought he'd be sampling the stuff for them.

Then there was the track star who was busted for using drugs, but was reinstated. He was fortunate enough to have hired a crack attorney.

Q: What is a cow's favorite Olympic event?
A: The herdles.

Q: What is an Olympic marathon?
A: An event in which a handful of superb athletes are watched by thousands of people who could really use the exercise.

Q: Why do so many Polish marathoners wear a Walkman when they train?

A: So they can listen to a tape that goes, "Left, right, left, right ..."

Then there was the Polish coach whose team came in dead last in the women's breaststroke events. She didn't realize the swimmers could use their arms.

Even worse was the mother of the Polish gold medalist. When her son brought the medal home, she promptly had it bronzed.

Q: What do you call an Olympic diving medalist who jumps into an unheated pool?

A: Greg Bluganis.

Q: What do you call him two days later?

A: Greg Fluganis.

Q: What's the difference between a group of stalking Pygmies and a women's track team?

A: One's a bunch of cunning runts. . . .

Coaches from around the world were headed to an Olympic seminar in Moscow when the airplane suddenly developed engine trouble.

"I've got some bad news," the pilot informed them. "Unless three of you jump, we'll never make it to the nearest airport."

Without hesitation, a Japanese coach went to the door, pulled it open, muttered, "Long live the emperor," and leaped to oblivion.

Encouraged by his example, a Lebanese coach went to the door, said, "Allah be praised," and jumped to his death.

Rising from his seat, a coach from Texas said, "Remember the Alamo," and threw a Mexican coach from the plane.

Q: Why is the Mexican summer Olympic team hurting so bad?
A: Because any Mexican who can swim, run, or jump is in the United States.

Q: Why aren't there any lepers in the slalom?
A: By the time they get to the top, they lose their nerve.

The studly young Mexican runner walked into a bar in L.A. during the Olympics. The woman tending bar recognized him from TV and knew that he was only seventeen.

"Pour me a cold one," said the runner.

She shook her head. "You wanna get me in trouble?"

"Maybe later," he replied. "Right now, I want a beer."

"Did you hear?" one Chinese diver said to another. "Chen died after losing the gold medal to an American."

"Died!" he shouted. "When?"

"Tomorrow."

Q: What's the one food all marathoners should eat?
A: Ketchup.

During the Olympics in Mexico, two highly competitive runners met for the first time in months.

"Hey," said the friendlier of the two, "how's your ass?"

"Shut up!" snapped the other.

The first said, "Mine too. Must be the water."

Roger Long had a unique way of training for the dashes in the Olympics: He would pit himself against horses, cars, motorcycles, and other speedsters in order to boost his speed.

It was a week before the games were to begin, and dissatisfied with his progress, he decided to train against a leopard. Flying to Africa, he went to a veldt with his trainers and found a leopard.

Standing in the tall grasses and waving his arms frantically, Roger caught the leopard's attention. While his trainers watched from a tall tree, the man raced the pursuing leopard.

"Can you see who's won?" one trainer asked the other.

"The winner is indeed spotted."

"Who was it?"

The other trainer replied, "I just told you."

Then there was the would-be track and field medalist who underwent a sex-change operation. Seems one hurdle was a tad higher than he thought it would be. . . .

Looking to boost her potassium levels before the Olympics, the runner asked her doctor, "Are bananas healthful?"

The physician replied, "I should say so! In twenty years, I've never had to treat one."

Te Song was the lowest, dirtiest marathoner in Olympics history. The Japanese runner would do anything to win, as his archrival Jim Trupin learned.

The two were in a dead heat as they neared the end of the race, and when Trupin began to pull ahead, the enraged Song stuck out his foot and tripped him. Although Song was disqualified, Trupin broke his ankle.

Four years later, Te Song wasn't permitted to enter the Olympics, and Trupin could not, his leg having been permanently damaged in the fall. As he bitterly described his lot to one sports columnist, "Te Song is gone, but the malady lingers on."

The Polish track star missed the team plane to the Olympics, so he ran to catch a commercial flight.

"I need a round-trip ticket!" he shouted to the woman at the ticket counter.

"Yes, sir. Where to?"

The athlete replied, "Back here, of course!"

One Olympic attendee said to another, "Didja hear about the Russian weight lifter who died while he was drinking milk?"

"Really? What happened?"

"He got a cramp and the cow fell on top of him."

Q: What's the one good thing about being a Greek athlete?

A: You never miss phone calls by being in the bathtub.

"Hear about the Turkish swimmer who defected to Iran?" one Olympics fan asked another. "He raised the average IQ of both teams."

After her Olympic victory, the young Polish gymnast went to the locker room and began undressing.

"Reporters want to talk to you," her trainer said.

"They'll have to wait," she said. "My papa told me never to be seen in public in my underwear."

The trainer went out and told the reporters the gymnast would be there soon. A moment later the athlete stepped out, naked as a babe.

Then there was Romek, the young Polish boy who wanted to be an Olympic swimmer.

"The most important thing to remember," said the trainer, "is never to swim on a full stomach."

Wanting to do everything he was told, the boy jumped right in after lunch and did the backstroke.

Q: How does Mark Spitz get to work each day?
A: Car pool.

Q: How did the crowd of Polish Olympic fans die?
A: They went to a track meet and were run over by a train.

Q: What happened when the diver missed the pool and hit the concession stand?
A: Nothing. He landed in a soft drink.

Then there were the Polish athletes whose equipment was lost in customs, so they made a deal to share a bobsled with the Russians. The Soviets had it going down-course, the Poles going up.

Another Polish athlete decided to switch events at the last minute: he went from the swimming to the broad jump when he heard it was a leap year. . . .

Yet another Polish athlete accepted a bet from a Russian athlete, who claimed he could jump across the river. When the bets were placed, the Russian swam to the other side and leaped.

The Pole paid up.

Polish athlete Rose Rosensky came home with a gold medal in broad jumping.

"It's amazing," said a reporter who met her at the airport. "To think that you spent years practicing the hammer throw, and you won this!"

"It was nothing, really," said the athlete.

"Nothing? It's a miracle! Tell me, how did you do it?"

"Simple," she said. "There I was, about to throw, when all of a sudden I backed into some fool's javelin—"

Then there was the Polish wrestling team, which arrived in the United States for an Olympic bout. While driving to the meet, they saw a sign that said ARENA LEFT, so they turned around and went home.

The wrestling team finally made it to the match, during which Grabowski injured his groin. The doctor told him to drink plenty of orange juice after a hot bath.

Later that day, the physician called to find out how he was.

"Are you drinking the orange juice?" the doctor asked.

"Gimme a break," said the Pole. "I've still got half the bath to drink."

Q: Why did the voyeur bust into the locker room where the vivacious Roman gymnast was getting ready?

A: He had a weakness for a zesty Italian dressing.

The Russian lady wrestler weighed in.

"One hundred seventy-two," said the official. "And the other leg's the same."

Q: Why is the super-restrictive passport for Chinese Olympic stars known as "American Express."

A: Because they don't leave home without it.

Q: What multisport event has been created for particularly high-strung athletes?

A: The decaffelon.

Then there was the Polish gymnast who tried to do a handstand. She broke all ten fingers when she stepped on them.

The ten-year-old Russian gymnast walked up to her trainer during lunch break.

"Excuse me, ma'am, but I'm writing a letter home, and I want to know: is there a hyphen in hard on?"

The woman nearly spit up her tea.

"Serafina—why do you want to know something like *that*?"

The girl replied, "I'm writing to tell my parents that I finally mastered that somersault we worked so hard on."

To make certain that there was nothing to distract or upset Olympic participants, the Polish Olympic committee decreed that no married athletes would be allowed to try out for the games.

Valya and Josef were distraught.

"Can't we keep it a secret?" Josef asked.

"But Josef," said Valya, "what if I get pregnant?"

Josef thought for a moment, then said, "We won't tell the baby either."

Then there was the down-and-out Australian who tried to get boomerang throwing into the Olympics. He was hoping to make a comeback . . .

. . . and the gymnastic hopeful who worked day and night on the high bar, but simply couldn't get the hang of it. . . .

More sinister were the Middle Eastern terrorists who plotted to assassinate the infidel who'd won the gold in the men's downhill. As their superiors put it, they were to "Eliminate the medal man."

Q: What's the difference between an obscene man and an Olympic fencer?
A: There is none. Both are sordid.

Q: What's the best way to describe the effort of a fencer who accidentally stabs another through the chest?
A: Halfhearted.

Q: Why was the track-and-field star nicknamed "Dress"?
A: Because she was a real long jumper.

Q: What does Pierre Quinon's event have in common with the safe in which the Gallup people store their data?
A: One's a pole vault, the other a poll vault.

Then there was the Polish athlete who practiced his handwriting day and night so he'd have a chance of winning the pentathlon . . .

. . . and the Polish lepidopterist who rushed to the Olympics when he heard there was a hundred-meter butterfly . . .

. . . and the Polish mother who pulled her son out of the Olympic trials and made him join the navy when his coach said the boy was fleet-footed . . .

... and the Polish track-and-field star who stayed up all night studying for her urine test. ...

Q: What's the difference between idealistic young athletes and those who make it to the Olympics?
A: The idealists shun drugs and hope to be discovered. The Olympic athletes use them and hope they aren't.

After being humiliated by showing up a week late for the games in Seoul in 1988, the Polish track-and-field team resolved that that wouldn't happen again in 1992. They made sure of the date and time of the meets, made reservations on a flight that would get them there with time to spare, and even sent their gear ahead to make certain it arrived.

Sure enough, the Polish team arrived on time. In Seoul.

On the eve of the summer games, the gym teacher asked the bookish Wordsworth, "Can you name five different kinds of Olympic athletes?"

"Most certainly," said the kid. "A boxer and five skaters."

Q: What does an Olympic fencing hopeful do at noon each day?
A: Leaves his office and goes out to lunge.

RODEO

The rodeo entourage was going to play Montreal. As soon as they stepped off the plane, the cowboys saw a sign that warmed them; in fact, the instant they checked into the hotel, they went out to do as they'd been invited: DRINK CANADA DRY.

Q: What drug have bulls been taking to make them bigger, stronger, and able to toss riders a mile?
A: Steeroids.

Q: Why don't rodeo riders ever clean their ears?
A: Because their heads would collapse.

Q: Why do so many rodeo riders chew tobacco?
A: To sweeten their breath.

Q: How can you tell when a rodeo rider is swearing?
A: His lips are moving.

Q: What's a wrench?
A: Where Israeli rodeo riders practice.

Michael Alexanderski left Warsaw for the United States, determined to become the greatest Polish rodeo rider in history. Impressed by his eagerness, the owner of the top traveling show decided to train him. On Michael's first day there, a cowboy took him aside to begin showing him the ropes.

"This here's a lariat or a riata," he said. "We use it to catch the cows."

Michael stroked his chin. "Very interesting. And what do you use for bait?"

Michael managed to make it through the first day, after which he decided to unwind. Hearing what the rest of the boys were going to do, he followed them to the local saloon. In his hand was a bucket and a canvas sack.

When he reached the tavern, he ordered two beers then overturned the bucket. A pile of manure slid out. Michael then reached into his pocket, pulled out a derringer, and shot the mound. Next, he opened the bag, released a kitten, and pursued the small animal around the room. It finally managed to slink out through an open window.

When Michael returned to his seat, the bartender stared at him, aghast.

"What in hell was that all about?" he asked.

The Pole shrugged. "I'm just doing what everyone else said they'd be doing."

"And what's that?"

"Drink a few beers, shoot the shit, and chase a little pussy."

Q: What term describes a rodeo that sells off its young cows?
A: Decalfinated.

Because the cowboy had joined the rodeo when he was ten, he never got a chance to finish high school. Deciding to take a correspondence course, he found the work load overwhelming and had no choice but to cut classes: he sent in empty envelopes.

Cowboy Curt worked for the rodeo. When his favorite horse broke a leg, he refused to let the rodeo owner shoot it. Instead, Curt and the animal worked a rodeo sideshow attraction that offered $1,000 to anyone who could make the stallion Rossinante laugh.

One day, a man walked over and said, "You

might as well give me the G-note, 'cause I'm gonna make your horse split a gut laughin'."

Curt watched intently as the man walked over to the horse and whispered something into its ear. A moment later, just as the man had predicted, the horse was hysterical.

Curt paid him the $1,000, then decided he'd better change the challenge. After all, if Rossinante was going to start laughing, the attraction would soon go broke.

The next day, Curt was offering $1,000 to anyone who could make the horse cry without touching him. To his dismay, the same man showed up bright and early.

"Get the grand ready," the man said, "because in about ten seconds, your horse's gonna be blubberin' like a baby."

His fingers crossed, Curt watched as the man walked around to the other side of the horse, where he couldn't see him.

"You can't hurt him—" Curt warned.

"I won't touch him," the man shouted.

A moment later, the horse began to cry uncontrollably. The cowboy came over, his hand outstretched. Curt began counting out hundred-dollar bills.

"You earned the money, stranger," Curt said, "but I have to know—how did you make Rossinante laugh yesterday and cry today?"

"Well," said the man, "yesterday, I told yer horse my penis was bigger 'n his. Today, I showed him."

Later that week, Curt was given another retired horse to care for, only this was a *very* special one: it could talk.

Seeing money to be made, Curt took this horse to the local bar. He boasted that the horse could talk, and the patrons gave him five-to-one odds that he couldn't.

After the bets had been placed, Curt told the horse to speak.

The horse just stood there, silent.

Curt urged him again, but still the horse remained mute. Dejected, he walked the animal from the bar.

As soon as they were outside, Curt screamed, "You bonehead! Why'd you do that? We could've made a fortune!"

"Hush up," said the horse. "Tomorrow we come back and get ten-to-one."

The promiscuous cowboy walked into the doctor's office in a small town on the rodeo tour.

"Doc, you got anything to cure crabs?" he asked.

"Maybe," replied the physician. "Depends what's ailin' them."

Upon being thrown from a bronco, Carson hurt his back so badly that he had to be wheeled into the doctor's office on a stretcher.

After looking at him, the doctor raised the

blinds and asked the nurse to wheel him over to the window.

"Crank the stretcher up so that he's vertical," the doctor said.

The nurse did as he asked.

"Now stick out your tongue nice and long," the doctor told the cowboy.

"Wh-what will that tell you?" the rider asked.

The doctor replied, "Nothing. I just can't stand my neighbors."

Q: What do you get when you cross a rodeo rider with an ape?
A: You still get an ape.

Q: What do you get when you cross a rodeo rider with a snake?
A: Trick question! Even snakes have standards.

Q: Why did the rodeo manager marry the sheep?
A: He had to.

In order to drum up business, the rodeo situated on the Mexican border introduced bull-fighting. As an added attraction, a booth was set up that served the testicles of the bull that was killed in the most recent event.

Each weekend for two years, rancher Hank Crockett went to the booth and feasted on the delicacies. However, one day he noticed that the portions were unusually small.

Hank complained to the grillman, who said apologetically, "Meester—it isn't always *el toro* who loses."

Q: What do you call a rodeo rider with half a brain?
A: Gifted.

The wrangler walked up to the new rider before the show.

"Say, podner," he said, "you're only wearing one spur."

"Nacherly," said the rider. "Whichever way one side o' the horse goes, t'other's gotta follow."

Q: What do you call it when cowboys go sculling?
A: Rowdeo.

Q: What do you call a rodeo rider's index finger?
A: A handkerchief.

The wrangler walked up to the new Polish rider, who was getting ready to ride a bucking bronco.

"Hey, bub," said the wrangler, "you're putting the saddle on backward."

The Pole replied, "How do you know which direction he'll be going?"

Q: How can you tell if a rodeo rider is educated?
A: There are no misspellings in his tattoo.

Q: What's the worst thing about falling off a bucking bronco?
A: First you're derided by the horse, then by the fans.

Then there was the rider who joined the rodeo with a tenderfoot rating. After a day in the saddle, it was a little higher than that.

That evening, the same tenderfoot was standing with another rider, watching a stunt woman perform.

"She's a great one," said the other rider. "She can go from riding on top of the horse to riding on the side of the horse with no problem."

"Big deal," said the tenderfoot. "I've been doing that all day."

After watching the tenderfoot make his debut, the wrangler walked up to him.

"Son," he said, "some riders are good and some are lousy, but you're both—good and lousy."

SAILING

The psychologist was invited to a local women's club to give a talk about sex. Certain his wife wouldn't be happy with him discussing such a personal topic in front of a group of women, he told her he was going to address them about sailing.

A few days after the talk, the psychologist's wife happened to bump into one of the women who was at the meeting.

"Splendid talk your husband gave the other night," the woman said.

The woman thanked her, then remarked, "I still don't understand why they asked him."

"Nonsense! He was extremely well informed."

"But he's only tried it twice. The first time he slipped on a wet spot while he was getting in, and the second time he got nauseous and threw up."

Q: Why are there so few Vietnamese yachtsmen?
A: It's tough to enjoy yourself with hundreds of people on the boat.

Q: What's the difference between a boat that never tilts and one that never moves.

A: None. They're both listless.

Q: What was the name of the vessel that won the first-ever yacht race held in the horse latitudes?

A: Seattle Slue.

One Nevadan said to another, "I wish I had the money to buy a sixty-foot sailboat."

His friend said, "We're landlocked. What would you do with a sailboat?"

"Nothing. I just wish I had the money."

Before embarking on his solo sailboat trip around the world, Harvey went to see his attorney.

"In case I die," said Harvey, "I'd like to leave everything to my wife."

"Of course."

"However, there is one stipulation. My wife must remarry within six months."

The lawyer scratched her head. "Why do you want to insist on that?"

Harvey replied, "I want somebody to be sad that I died."

Harvey added one more request to his will.

"If my body is ever found, I wish to be buried at sea."

"Because of your love for sailing?" asked the lawyer.

Harvey shook his head. "Because my wife always swore she'd dance on my grave."

Then there was the Pole who was banned from America's Cup competition for cheating. Wanting desperately to be part of the race, he waited until the competition was about to begin, then put on a disguise and tunneled his way onto the Polish vessel. . . .

In light of that fiasco, Polish yachtsmen decided to establish a race of their own. And they felt they improved on the America's Cup, in fact, by announcing that the competition would be held indoors in the event of rain. . . .

Q: What's the best way to describe a beached yacht?
A: Hull on earth.

Q: After a near collision with another ship, the shaken captain went below. What did he leave on the bridge?
A: A log.

Then there was the shipyard that underwent a name change because the boat race was coming to town. It's now called Yachts of Luck. . . .

The shipyard also sold spare hawser lines, which they advertised with a billboard that read GIVE YOUR BUSINESS TO US—HAVE-KNOTS.

Q: How many yachtsmen does it take to screw in a light bulb?
A: None. They screw in their staterooms.

Q: What did yachtsmen call the *Stars and Stripes* after Dennis Conner added huge tail fins?
A: A caddymaran.

Q: What kind of propulsion system did Conner add that sent the vessel soaring through the air?
A: A catapult.

SKIING

Q: Why did the Pole sell his water skis?
A: He couldn't find any lakes on the ski slope.

The young woman walked into the lodge clothing shop.

"Got anything that will go with my lilac and fawn outfit?"

The salesclerk looked her up and down. "Might I suggest a trench coat?"

Whitney said to her friend, "You know, I used to ski for days on end."

"What happened?" asked the friend.

"My husband taught me how to keep my balance."

The ski lodge was honoring Mrs. Chaney for thirty years of service at the reservations desk. Ski instructor Talbot was in charge of getting the gift, and he'd spent a small fortune on a bottle of hundred-year-old Pinot Noir Burgundy.

Talbot drove up to the lodge on the night of the party, and to protect the bottle from the cold, he tucked it inside his coat.

As he walked to the building, he heard someone yelling nearby: he turned just as one of the world's worst skiers came tumbling off a slope. The skier collided with Talbot, and they both fell hard to the ground.

As the skier scampered to his feet, apologizing profusely, Talbot lay there, feeling something wet spreading along his waistband.

"All I've got to say," said Talbot through his teeth, "is that that had better be blood!"

Then there was the sage who pointed out that skiing was a lot like sex. When it's good, it's wonderful, and when it's bad, it still beats just about anything else.

Q: Why didn't the skier mind turning sixty-five?
A: She heard it was all downhill from there.

The boy was so busy acting cool, he didn't see the little girl on the slopes until he ran into her.

The girl's irate father came storming over.

"You little punk!" the man screamed. "I'll teach you to run over other children!"

"Don't bother," said the boy, picking himself up and hurrying away. "I did a pretty good job without lessons."

During an unexpected March thaw, the Pole showed up at the resort to do some skiing.

"But we don't have any snow," said the man at the ski lift.

The Pole insisted, but the man refused to take him up. Still, the Pole argued.

"Look," said the exasperated lodge employee, "I don't know why you aren't getting the message, but let's try it this way. If you took the 'ball' out of 'football,' what would you have?"

"Foot," said the Pole.

"And if you took the 'base' out of 'baseball,' what would that leave you?"

"Ball," the Pole replied.

"And if you took the 'fuck' out of 'snow,' what would you have?"

The Pole thought for a moment, then said, "There is no fuck in snow."

The employee said, "Exactly."

Q: Because his name ended in "ski," what sport did the Pole take up?
A: Skating.

Q: What was the motto of the Aspen lodge owner who went to Hollywood and drummed up business by promising to pamper movie stars?
A: "There's snow business like show business."

Q: What do they call tinsel-bedecked bumps on ski runs?
A: Movie moguls.

Q: How can you pick out a Polish skier on the slopes?
A: He's the one with snow chains on his skis.

Then there was the Polish skier who got a severe case of frostbite on his legs. He couldn't figure out how to put on his pants over his skis.

Q: How do you recognize a Pole in a car wash?
A: He's the one with the skis on his ski rack.

Q: How many Poles does it take to wax skis?
A: Two. One to hold the wax, the other to move the skis back and forth.

Q: What's nearly as important to skiers as fine, white snow?
A: Good Blue Cross.

Q: What's the difference between skiing and going to a singles' bar?
A: At the singles' bar, if you run into someone of the opposite sex, you may end up in love. On the slopes, if you run into someone of the opposite sex, you may end up in traction.

The young man went to confession.

"Father—forgive me, for I have sinned. I was on the slopes last week when I happened to see my boss standing off to the side. He didn't see me, so I hid my face in my scarf, skied over, poked him with my pole, and laughed as he tumbled down the hill."

"But my son," said the priest, "this is the seventh time you've confessed the sin."

"I know," said the young man. "I just like talking about it."

Then there was the skier who was out for hours on end. She finally decided to take lessons. . . .

SKYDIVING

Skydiving is the only sport in the world where, if something goes wrong, they have to dig you up to bury you . . .

. . . unless, of course, you're one of those do-it-yourself skydivers who jumps over Forest Lawn. . . .

Q: What kind of music is played at a skydiver's funeral?
A: A R.I.P. chord.

Q: Why did the women of the nude skydiving team decide to wear panties?
A: They were self-conscious about the way they whistled on the way down.

Q: What's the difference between a 747 and skydiving?
A: The 747: airplane. Skydiving: air playin'.

Penelope went skydiving for the first time and was enjoying it quite a bit—until she pulled her ripcord. The parachute failed to deploy, and in a panic, she pulled the cord on her emergency chute. It too failed to open.

Sobbing, certain that she was about to die, Penelope noticed a man soaring *toward* her from the ground. The woman didn't care how or why he was there, but began maneuvering toward him, hoping he could pull open the chute.

The man continued rising, she kept falling, and when they were within shouting distance, Penelope cried out, "Sir—do you know how to fix a parachute?"

The man shouted back, "Not really ... but I *can* tell you how not to fix a gas oven!"

Then there were the skydivers who were nearly over their target when they started arguing about the correct way to fold a parachute. Turns out they were both wrong, and as the pilot later put it, the two had a terrible falling-out. . . .

Timothy decided to try his hand at skydiving. "The most important thing to remember about jumping from an airplane," said the instructor, "is to pull the ripcord after counting to ten."

Timothy raised his hand. "Exc-c-cuse m-m-me, b-b-but what n-n-number was th-that again?"

The instructor said, "Three."

Q: What do you call a group of Polish sky-divers?
A: Air pollution.

Then there was the Polish inventor who came up with a fail-proof parachute. It opens on impact.

Stosh and Yosh jumped from the plane at 10,000 feet. Much to Yosh's horror, his harness broke and his parachute went tumbling away.

Stosh worked his way over.

"We'll share my chute!" he yelled, and pulled the ripcord.

True to his word, as soon as they passed the 5,000-foot level, he removed the chute and gave it to his friend.

Then there was the skydiving student who didn't pay attention when she packed her chute, and jumped to a conclusion . . .

. . . and the skydiving instructor who noted that the only way to truly master the sport was to throw yourself into it . . .

... and the other instructor who pointed out that skydiving wasn't as dangerous as it seemed.

"In the entire history of skydiving," she said, "no one has ever had more than one accident ..."

SOCCER

Q: Traditionally, who are the most indispensable men in international soccer competition?
A: The riot control police.

The World Cup game between Poland and a very hostile Spanish team quickly resulted in a brawl of unprecedented ferocity. As a result, the entire Spanish team was disqualified.

Toward the end of the second half, the Polish team scored the winning goal.

Q: Why is the new soccer stadium in Cracow an unmitigated disaster?
A: No matter where you sit, you're behind a Pole.

Thrilled when his team won the World Cup, the goalie decided to throw a party. And as a special honor, he asked the team's coach to say grace.

Clearing his throat, the coach rose and offered a small prayer, which he concluded by saying, ". . . we thank you, Lord, in the name of the Father, the Son, and the goalie host."

The girl came home after her first soccer practice.

"How'd you enjoy it?" her father asked.

"It was okay," she said, "but I'd have liked it better if the other team learned to share!"

Sitting in the grandstand waiting for the game to begin, Bertram turned to a total stranger.

"Bet you five dollars that before the game begins I can tell you the score."

The stranger was a gambling man, so he took the bet.

After they'd handed the bills to another fan, the gambler said, "Go ahead, big shot. Tell me the score."

Bertram replied, "Zero-zero."

After practice, one player walked over to his Polish teammate.

"Odd shoes you're wearing, one white and the other blue."

"Not odd at all," replied the Pole. "In fact, I've got another pair just like 'em at home."

The elementary-school coach called the little goalie over to him.

"Sally," he said, "in this league, we don't believe in swearing or taunting the other players. Do you understand that?"

"Of course, sir."

"Good. Then would you mind going to the grandstand and explaining it to your dad?"

College captain Kaplan had been given an ultimatum: if teammate Burk couldn't count past five, he wouldn't be allowed to play in the championship match. The captain tutored him hard; now, before the game, he showed the sole of his shoe to Burk.

"How many studs in this shoe, Claude?"

Claude scratched his head. "Duh ... just one."

The flattered captain had to let him play.

During his sermon, the priest asked, "Raise your hands—how many of you want to go to heaven?"

The clergyman looked out on the sea of upraised arms, then noticed that little Tanya's hands were folded in her lap.

"Miss Michaelson," the preacher said angrily, "you didn't raise your hand. Don't you want to go to heaven?"

"Oh yes," she replied, "but I don't want to miss my soccer game at two."

Q: Why did the Russian team install Astroturf in their stadium?
A: To keep the cheerleaders from grazing.

For the duration of the game, Roddy sat behind a pole at the soccer stadium, unable to see much of what was happening on the field.

When he went home and told his wife about the terrible seat he'd had, she asked, "Why didn't you ask the person next to you to switch for a while?"

"I couldn't," Roddy said. "There was no one in it."

Then there was the high-school soccer player who was left back.

Q: Where do Scotsmen dress for a soccer match?
A: Loch-er room.

Q: Why was Cinderella picked last for the Fairyland soccer team?
A: She had a habit of running from the ball.

Noah and his animals decided to have a soccer match on the ark, with Noah coaching one team, and his wife coaching another.

The game was a heated one, and was tied with

just seconds to go. Finally, a centipede got the ball for Noah's team, raced across the field, and scored.

Running over to congratulate the insect athlete, Noah said, "That was a brilliant run, but where the hell were you the rest of the game?"

The centipede replied, "I was puttin' on my sneakers."

Q: What do you call it when a kid can't go to school because he broke his leg playing soccer?
A: A lame excuse.

Q: What's the difference between two dogs in love and a soccer player who put his socks on inside out?
A: There's no difference. You've got to turn the hose on both of them.

His arms laden with popcorn, hot dogs, and soda, the obese fan climbed the stands and stopped beside a woman sitting on the aisle.

"Madam," he said, "did I step on your feet when I left before?"

"You most certainly did!" she snapped.

"Good," he said as he squirmed in front of her. "This is my row."

Q: Why don't Polish soccer teams break for more than a minute between halves?
A: Because then all the players would have to be retrained.

Q: Why did the Polish soccer player put on a fresh uniform after his shower?
A: The one he had on got soaking wet.

Little Harold walked in the front door sobbing. "Th-the kids threw me off the soccer team!" he told his mother.

"Why in heaven's name did they do that?"

Harold said, "Because they finally got a real soccer ball."

SPORTSCASTERS

Q: What's the difference between a proctologist and an athlete being interviewed after a game?
A: The proctologist only has to deal with one asshole at a time.

Q: What do you need when you come across Howard Cosell buried to his chin in cement?
A: More cement.

Q: What's the difference between Howard Cosell and a pothole?
A: You'd swerve to avoid the pothole.

Q: What do you call three sportscasters sinking in quicksand?
A: A good start.

Horace was new at the sportscasting game, and he approached the wrestling match with some trepidation: his job was to interview Madman Muldoon before the contest ... the selfsame Muldoon who had chewed off one man's ear in the ring and ripped the little toe off another.

Madman came over accompanied by his manager. The big man was snorting and salivating for the cameras.

"Don't worry," the manager whispered to Horace. "Madman's really a pussycat. Why, he'll eat off your hand!"

Horace loosened his necktie and said, "That's just what I'm afraid of."

One of Howard Cosell's producers thought it would help the sportscaster remain calm if he had someone to talk to on the road, so he bought him a parrot. The bird was indeed a comfort and joy, as it repeated everything Howard said.

One day, Howard was in his hotel room, showering, and there was a knock on the door.

"Who is it?" the bird asked.

"Mr. Cosell sent for me. It's the manicurist."

"Who is it?"

"The manicurist."

"Who is it?" the bird asked again.

"I said, it's the *manicurist,* you fool!"

"Who is it?"

"THE MANICURIST!" the woman shouted—and promptly suffered a stroke and died.

A moment later, Cosell came out of the bathroom. He opened the front door to get the newspaper and saw the woman lying there.

"Who's this?" he asked.

"The manicurist," the bird replied.

It was spring training, and the sportscaster walked up to the new baseball coach, a man who was great in the bullpen but had been somewhat shortchanged upstairs.

"Coach," said the reporter, "according to the dope I heard in the other camps, your team's going to have trouble this year."

To which the coach replied, "That's bull, and I want the name of the dope who told you that!"

Then there was the sportscaster who pointed out that second stringers are a lot like blisters: they always appear after the hard work is done.

One-upping him was the sports columnist who described a basketball squad's wretched loss as "A team *F* fort."

After the basketball team's devastating loss, the sportscaster asked the coach, "What do you think of your team's execution tonight?"

Without hesitation, the coach answered, "Frankly, I think it's an excellent idea."

Then there was the sportscaster who said that baseball was the easiest game to call.

"The only requirement," said he, "is that you know hits, know runs, and know errors."

Veronica, a beautiful young woman, went to the cigar-smoking producer, intent on becoming a sportscaster at all costs.

He watched her tape, chatted with her a bit, then took her out to dinner. After that, they went back to his apartment.

"Do you really think I have a chance of making it big?" she finally asked.

"Miss," he replied, "you're already making it big."

Veronica was thrilled when the producer called and informed her she'd been hired. As she told her closest friend, she was made for the job. . . .

When the pitcher was transferred from the Dodgers to the Mets, the sportscaster asked, "What do you think of Flushing, New York?"

The pitcher replied, "Great idea."

Q: How many sportscasters does it take to change a light bulb?

A: Two. One to change it, the other to do color.

The rather long-winded sportscaster was retiring, and his colleagues threw him a party. Much to everyone's chagrin, after the meal the announcer got up to say a few words.

Two hours later, he was still at it.

". . . and I want to state here and now," he said, "that the integrity with which we approach our work not only serves the public, but will set an example for the sportscasters who come after us—"

At which point an exhausted partygoer shouted, "And do you intend to keep talking till they get here?"

The Easter Bunny, an unabrasive sportscaster, and a lady of the evening were walking down the street when they spotted a hundred-dollar bill. Which one of them got to keep it?

The lady of the evening did. The other two are creatures of myth.

Remember Veronica? Seems she was chronically late for work, and the producer finally went up to her after a taping.

"We may have been lovers," he said to her, "but who says you can show up whenever you feel like it?"

She smiled sweetly. "My attorney."

Then there was the British sportscaster who noted that Prince Charles is so smitten with polo that only once did he go more than two days without playing—and that was on his honeymoon.

"And do you happen to know where he spent it?" he asked his listeners. "Why, In-Diana, I've heard."

As part of the exchange program that brought the British sportscaster to the United States, an American went to England to cover sports there. During his very first report, though, he raised eyebrows by reporting, "Rugby is a game played by men with oddly shaped balls."

In Milwaukee to cover a basketball game, announcer Albert Marvin was told that he'd have to come up with something to fill ten minutes of airtime before the game.

In a quandary, Al ran to the locker room and asked the coach if he could borrow a couple of Bucks. . . .

Alas, the Milwaukee coach turned Al down, so the desperate announcer ran over to the Miami bench to get some players. There, he discovered, to his chagrin, that he couldn't take the Heat. . . .

So, quick like a bunny, Al called around and asked to do a phone interview with any available players. The response was Knicks.

Unfortunately for announcer Al, not only was he given a player with whom he was unfamiliar, but the man was dumber than toast.

"Your name is—"

"Sanford," said the player.

"I mean, what's your whole name?" Al pressed. The player thought for a moment, then answered, "Anus."

Then there was the Polish sportscaster who refused to be on AM radio, because he didn't get up until early in the afternoon . . .

. . . and the famous baseball announcer who hailed from the small town of Nohitsnorunsno, Ariz. . . .

Nearly as famous was the Astros announcer who was born in Swingana, Miss. . . .

. . . and the rude newspaper reporter who offended the owner of a ball club and found himself depressed. . . .

The technician received a tongue-lashing from the director.

"How come you weren't there for Cosell's last broadcast?"

The technician replied, "Hell, if I'da known it was his last broadcast, I wouldn't'a missed it!"

"And listen," the seasoned New York sports-caster told the intern, "whatever you do, don't confuse the Mets, Nets, and Jets. They're confused enough as is."

Q: What's the difference between Howard Cosell and the pope?
A: The people who work for the pope only have to kiss his ring.

The junior executive walked up to a beautiful young woman at the network Christmas party.

"Can you believe that asshole?" he said, gesturing toward a sportscaster holding court in the corner. "Thinks he knows everything about sports. Christ, he couldn't predict the Super Bowl winner the day after the game."

The woman glared at him. "Do you know who I am, young man?"

The executive shook his head.

"I'm that 'asshole's' daughter!"

The executive stood tall. "And do you know who I am?"

The woman said icily, "I do not."

"Thank God," he said as he hurried away, "my job's safe."

The know-it-all sportscaster had just finished trashing a batter for hitting into a triple play. His colleague in the booth, a former major league player, said on the air, "Howard—you're so smart, is it true you were one of the Three Wise Men who followed the Star of Bethlehem?"

"Not so," said Howard.

The other announcer was stunned by this burst of modesty.

Howard explained, "I was the little one in the manger."

As it happened, Howard died the very next day. He was out taking his morning constitutional when a motorboat hit him.

Q: What did the sportscaster say after calling Mike Tyson's right jab "ineffective" . . . to his face?

A: It beats me!

The sportscaster made his way to the loser's corner after the big bout with Mike Tyson.

"What's in the future for you?" the reporter asked.

"Well," said the fighter, "I think I'm going to give up this game. Two fights with Tyson are enough—"

"Two?" said the sportscaster. "My good fellow, you only fought the champ once."

"Wrong," said the challenger. "I fought him twice tonight: for the first and last time."

The sportscaster was standing on the sidelines at the football game, using headphones to listen to instructions from the control booth. However, two chatty cheerleaders behind him were making that difficult.

He finally turned and snarled, "Ladies, please! I can't hear a thing!"

"And why should you?" one replied. "This is none of your business."

Watching the marathon, the sportscaster was aghast when Trudy, the woman in first place, actually slowed down to casually try and trip Sarah, the woman who was gaining on her.

"Sarah's a little behind," the sportscaster summed it up, "but Trudy's a big one!"

Yet, if athletes can sometimes be obnoxious, it's also true that many sportscasters are detested for being oft-spoken. . . .

Then there was the sage who pointed out that Howard Cosell may be outspoken . . . but he had no idea by whom.

And a tip of the hat to the Japanese businessman who bought his son a remote sportscasting unit: ABC.

SURFING

A beach bum stopped beside some kids who were looking longingly at the breakers.

"So you dream of surfing," said the bum.

"Man, do we!" said one.

The bum smiled. "Let me tell you a little story. A couple of years ago, I dreamed of catching the perfect wave. But I got cocky one day and decided to do a handstand while I rode a small wave in. I fell, the board hit me on the head, and my balance went all to hell. I haven't been able to ride since. Any questions?"

There was a deep silence, until one of the kids said, "Dude—can I have the board?"

Q: Why do so few Hawaiian women surf?
A: They're afraid of being harpooned.

The reporter asked the surfer, "Do you happen to know in which competition the famous Dave 'Big Wednesday' Keaton lost his life?"

"Sure, man," the surfer nodded. "His last."

Little Tony went to the beach with his mother. Trying to imitate the surfers he'd seen, the boy grabbed a slab of wood, carried it out to sea, and tried to surf. Unaccustomed to the waves, he went under and would have drowned had it not been for the quick actions of a lifeguard.

Tony was taken to the nearest doctor, and after hours, the lifeguard came to see how he was.

As the youth walked in, Tony's mother turned and looked up at him.

"Are you the young man who pulled my Tony from the ocean?" she asked.

"Yes, ma'am."

She frowned. "He had a cap."

Q: What kind of surfers do you find in the Arctic Ocean?
A: Cold ones.

The surfer and the horseback rider spent their lives arguing whose sport was more enjoyable. Finally, both of them passed on, the surfer going to heaven, the rider going to hell.

One day, they happened to meet at an afterlife picnic.

"How're the waves in heaven?" asked the rider.

"Not good," said the surfer. "God doesn't like the noise the big breakers make, so he keeps the waves small. How about you? How's the riding down below?"

"Great!" said the equestrian. "The devil's horses all have spirit! I actually have to slow them down from time to time."

Moral: It's better to rein in hell than to surf in heaven.

Q: Why did the surfer cross the sea?
A: To get to the other tide.

After riding a massive wave, the experienced surfer said to a novice, "Man, doesn't an experience like that make you glad to be alive?"

The novice replied, "No. Amazed."

The teenager went to the whorehouse and asked to see a woman who had VD. Though the madam was surprised, she did as the customer asked.

A week later, she bumped into him at a pizza parlor.

"How are you feeling?" she asked.

"Okay," he said. "I went to the doctor and got my shots."

"I see," said the madam. "I don't mean to pry, but I never had anyone ask for a girl with the clap before. Why did you do that?"

"Because I wanted to infect the maid."

"The maid? Why?"

"So she'd give it to my old man, and then he'd give it to my mother."

Now the madam was thoroughly confused. "Why on earth did you want to give your mother VD?"

"So she'd give it to the UPS man. He's the bastard who ran over my new surfboard."

A photographer and a lawyer were out surfing when sharks were spotted offshore. The two men began paddling back to the beach, but the shark was too quick for them. It gobbled up the photographer, then moved toward the lawyer.

In desperation, the lawyer turned and said something to the shark; suddenly, the big man-eater turned and swam away. When the lawyer reached the shore, a lifeguard ran over.

"That was incredible!" he said. "I thought you were a goner."

"Incredible nothing. I told him I was a lawyer."

"That's why he spared you?"

The lawyer said, "Sure. Professional courtesy."

Q: Why did the surfer join the navy?
A: He heard that some of the WAVES were awesome.

Q: Why did they stop doing the Wave at Shea Stadium?
A: Too many Poles were bringing their surfboards.

Q: How do you make a Surfer Stew?
A: Steal his board.

Q: What do competitive surfers call the wave that wins them a championship?
A: A title wave.

Then there was the Pole who invented a training surfboard—one board for each foot . . .

. . . and the motel by the sea that appealed to out-of-town surfers by offering room and board. . . .

Q: How did the surfer feel after he lost his hairpiece in a fall?
A: He was dis-tressed.

While he was out surfing, Tad slipped, hit his head on the board, and was knocked unconscious. Seeing him slip under the waves, a seabird swooped down, grabbed his gold chain, and held his head above water until the lifeguard arrived.

The next day, Tad went to a pet store and bought the most beautiful seabird he could find. Taking it to the shore, he waited until he saw the bird that had rescued him, then set the bird free. The two fell in love instantly and flew off together.

"Why did you do that?" a bather asked.

"Simple," Tad replied. "One good tern deserves another."

A young Israeli surfer visited a friend in Malibu. After a morning of riding the waves, the two had lunch on the beach and watched the women walk by.

"So," said the surfer from Malibu, "what do you think of bathing beauties in America?"

He replied, "If they'll let me, I'll wash them anywhere."

And what would any joke book be without one of these:

Q: Why don't elephants surf?
A: They have trouble keeping their trunks up.

TENNIS

Q: After several long, exhausting games of tennis, what do lepers always forget to take from the showers?
A: Their head and shoulders.

Q: Why did the leper tennis player have to finish the match in a wheelchair?
A: She was de-feeted in the first set.

After scraping together the money for a vacation in Hawaii, Norm Koch was horrified to arrive at his hotel, the Wanarobia, and discover that the room was costing $300 a day. Though the price included all meals, the pool, a show, and free tennis, he couldn't afford to spend so much. So he dragged his luggage to the next hotel and was delighted to learn that the rooms were only $100 a night.

Settling in, he headed for the tennis court and went to buy some balls.

"That will be fifty dollars, sir," said the man at the counter.

"Fifty dollars!" Norm shrieked. "That's insane! Why, they're free at the Wanarobia!"

"That's true. But over there, they get you by the rooms."

Q: What do you call a tennis match between Ray Charles and Stevie Wonder?
A: Endless love.

Q: How can you tell when WASPs are in mourning?
A: They're wearing black tennis outfits.

Q: Why did the Polish boy wait until he reached puberty before taking up tennis?
A: He heard you couldn't play unless you had fuzzy balls.

While trying to return a powerful smash, Jonathan got in the way of the ball and it went down his throat. Miraculously, he didn't choke, and his opponent rushed him to the hospital.

There wasn't time to give Jonathan anything more than a local anesthetic, and he watched with some distress as the doctor made a cut in his stomach, then in his left side, next in his throat, and finally in his right side.

"Hey, doc," Jonathan wheezed, "why so many incisions?"

"Look," snapped the doctor, "that's the way the ball bounces!"

At lunchtime, Otto walked over to his Polish co-worker and said, "What would you say to a set of tennis."

Scratching his head, the Pole said, "Hello, set."

When she heard little Nancy cursing during jumprope, the schoolyard monitor hurried over.

"Now, now," the woman said, "you know what happens to little girls who say naughty words!"

"Yes," said Nancy. "They grow up and play tennis."

Nick ran onto the tennis court one Sunday morning.

"Why so late?" his opponent asked.

"I flipped a coin to decide whether to go to church or come here."

"Why should that take so long?"

Nick said, "I had to keep flipping till the coin got it right."

The young man walked up to the priest.

"Is it a sin to play tennis on Sunday?"

The priest replied, "The way you play, it's a sin any day."

The club pro watched as the priest served ball after ball into the net. Nothing the pro suggested could help the clergyman, and after a while, the priest began losing his temper, though he always stopped short of smashing the racket, kicking the balls, or swearing. Finally, the pro suggested they take a break.

"I'm giving it up," the priest said as they walked to the lounge.

"Tennis?"

"No," said the priest, "the church."

"So," the club's newest member asked the pro, "what do you think of my game?"

"Frankly, I still prefer tennis."

"How do you like my game?" Meredith asked the pro. "I spent nearly $5,000 on lessons."

"You ought to get to know my wife," said the pro.

"Oh? Is she a good player?"

"No," said the pro. "She's a lawyer."

Meredith was hurt by the pro's remarks, but she was also a realist.

"Are you saying that I'm the worst player you ever saw?" she asked.

"Not at all," said the pro.

Meredith beamed. "Well, that's encouraging."

The pro added, "but the others all had the decency to give up the game."

George and Peter walked up and down the courts, checking out who was playing, looking for a game of mixed doubles. Suddenly, George turned his back on a pair of women.

"What's the matter?" Peter asked.

"Over there—my wife and my mistress playing together!"

Peter looked at the women. "Hey, now that's a coincidence. They're mine too!"

Bentworth was offensively status conscious, but Nichols found a way to one-up him: He got a new portable phone designed especially to be carried in tennis bags.

As soon as he reached the court, Nichols punched in Bentworth's number.

"Old bean," Nicholas said, "guess where I'm calling from?"

"Two courts over," Bentworth said. "I saw you come in."

Nichols turned and, sure enough, there was Bentworth, playing two courts away and conversing on his own tennis-bag phone.

"So," Bentworth said, "you got some of these delightful toys too?"

Nichols tried not to show his disappointment, and consoled himself with the knowledge that at least he hadn't been one-upped. "Yes, it's a real necessity—"

"Hold on, would you?" Bentworth interrupted. "My other line is ringing."

A pair of New York dockworkers were vacationing in Southern California. While they were out playing tennis, one said to the other, "God—it's hot here, isn't it?"

"Of course it is," said his companion. "Are you forgetting how far we are from the ocean?"

The WASPish Richard burst into the infirmary at the racquet club.

"Quickly," he yelled, "I need smelling salts! My fiancée's fainted on the court."

The nurse handed them over. Richard uncapped the bottle and took a whiff.

"Thanks," he said, handing them back. "Seeing her go down like that really got to me."

Maurice strolled into the office at 1:00 P.M.

"Where'd you have lunch?" a co-worker asked.

"I didn't. I was playing tennis with my secretary."

"How nice. Score?"

Maurice winked. "Give me another day or two."

Gary was not only a superb tennis pro, he amazed the members of the club by his ability to sip a wine and tell them its vintage.

"Twenty-year-old Barbaresco," he said, tasting a red wine handed to him by a club member.

"Nine-year-old Chardonnay," he said, after

sampling a dry white wine provided by another member.

He took a third glass from a slightly inebriated man at the table beside theirs. After putting it to his lips, he spat violently.

"This tastes like piss!" he declared.

"Right," said the man. "Now, how old am I?"

Q: What is it called when one player bends to tie a shoe just as another serves?
A: An ace in the hole.

Wayne went to the pet store to buy a parrot. One bird caught his eye: previously owned, it was especially handsome and he purchased it. As soon as the bird was settled on its perch, Wayne went to the cupboard.

"Ace want a cracker?" he asked, holding out a Saltine.

The bird looked at the snack. "What are you, *stupid*? And *blind*? You think I keep my feathers rich by eating *crackers*, you moron? I want pâté and I want it *now*, asshole!"

Shocked by this unprovoked abuse, Wayne returned to the pet store and walked up to the proprietor.

"Just who owned that bird before me anyway?" he demanded.

"Didn't I tell you?" the proprietor said. "You are the owner of a bird that once belonged to John McEnroe."

The tennis pro was a curious one: every time he missed a shot, he stopped, looked up, and shouted, "Fanity! *Fanity!*"

Lester and Alton were playing on the next court.

"What the hell is he doing?" Lester asked.

"Imitating John McEnroe."

"McEnroe?"

"Sure. Don't you recognize pro-fanity when you hear it?"

Martha walked onto the tennis court and watched with amazement as a man and a cat played a vigorous round of tennis in the court next to hers.

After the game was finished, Martha walked over to the man as the cat lay down its racket and lapped water from a dish.

"I just wanted to tell you that your cat is the most incredible animal I've ever seen," Martha said.

"Bah," said the man, "not so incredible at all. I've whipped him two sets out of three."

"I don't know what's wrong with me!" the tennis star said to another between sets. "I can't return anything Martina is serving!"

"Suggestion," said the other player. "Stand close to the net when you swing."

"You think that'll help?"

The player shrugged. "If nothing else, Martina may catch a cold from the breeze."

"Heard about the new John McEnroe tennis racket?" one pro asked another.

"No. What about it?"

"If there's a bad call, it flies off the handle."

"Don't be intimidated by the player on the other side of the net," the trainer told the player before her first big match. "Remember: If she was any good, she wouldn't be playing you."

After a long day of tennis, new club member John bid adieu to longtime member Clark.

"No time for a shower?" Clark asked.

John flushed. "I've the time," he said, "but . . . well, I have a problem."

"Tell me about it," said Clark. "It's okay. I'm a psychiatrist."

"Well, the truth is . . . I've got a really short penis, and I'm sort of self-conscious about it."

"Has having a short penis hurt your sex life?" Clark asked.

"No, not at all. In fact, I can stay hard all night."

"Shit, John." Clark sighed. "How'd you like to swap it for one that looks great in the shower?"

Q: What's the oldest tennis game in recorded history?

A: It's written that Moses served in the Egyptian court.

Phil Smith went to see his physician.

"Doc, ya gotta help me. Every day at lunch hour, I have this incredible urge to play tennis. And if I go, I can't leave . . . it's like an addiction!"

The doctor thought for a moment, then wrote out a prescription.

Phil read it. "Put a fish in a blender, liquefy, and drink the contents every day at 11:59. Doc, this'll cure me?"

"No," said the physician, "but it'll make you so sick you won't want to play."

Then there was the tennis player who went to the doctor because he heard music whenever he played. The physician cured him by removing his headband.

One doctor phoned another.

"Forget the game we had planned for today."

"Why?" asked the other.

"Mr. Orlando just left here, and from the shape his joints are in, it's going to rain for sure."

The tennis pro bumped into his doctor at a cocktail party.

"Jeez," said the pro, "I'm sick of people cornering me after hours and asking for help with their serve, their backhand, their forehand."

"I have the same problem," the doctor replied, "only I have an advantage you don't. Whenever they start describing symptoms to me, I can send them away with two little words."

"Which are?" asked the pro.

"Kindly disrobe."

"The best advice I can give you for your elbow," said the doctor, "is to give up tennis."

"Aw, doc," said the tennis fanatic, "I just don't deserve the best. What's second best?"

The Japanese player's game was off, so he went to the ophthalmologist—even though he had precious little faith in doctors.

After giving the player a thorough examination, the eye doctor said, "Your problem, sir, is that you have a cataract."

The player laughed. "That's what you know! So happens I have a Rincoln."

When Benson started losing every game in his weekly match, he went to see a psychiatrist.

After listening to him, the analyst said, "Your

problem, my friend, is that you worry too much about the game. A few weeks ago, a man came in complaining about the same thing. I told him to relax, and as soon as he did his game improved."

"I know," said Benson. "He's my opponent."

Q: What do they call a tennis player's income?
A: Net earnings.

Dr. Tetch was addressing the class of aspiring psychiatrists.

"Let me tell you a little story," Tetch said. "When I was a boy, I only cared about one thing: tennis. I'd play after school, I'd play on weekends, and I'd even sneak out for night games.

"But there came a time when a professor at this school took me aside, appropriated my racket, and handed me a textbook. 'Read,' he said. 'Study. Learn.' I took his advice seriously, which is why I am what I am today."

A student stood and cheered, "One of the world's greatest psychiatrists!"

"No," said Dr. Tetch. "One of the world's worst tennis players."

After months of therapy, the psychiatrist said to the man, "You're cured. You no longer believe you're John McEnroe."

"Great," said the patient. "I can't wait to go home and give Tatum the good news!"

"Doc," said the tennis player, "I get this terrible pain in my shoulder every time I use my backhand. What should I do?"

The doctor replied, "Work on your serve and develop a hell of a forehand."

Then there was the doctor who prescribed tennis for insomniacs. It didn't help them sleep, but it wasn't such a drag to be awake.

It was Saturday morning, and Dr. Klein had reluctantly agreed to spend it with his wife.

Just as they were about to go shopping, the phone rang. It was Klein's colleague, Dr. Herman.

"Listen," said Herman, "I'm with Dr. Xavier and Dr. Lao. We need a fourth for doubles. Can you make it?"

"Hmm," said Klein. "Uh-huh ... yes, I see. I'll be right over." He hung up and grabbed his medical kit. "Sorry, dear," he said, "but I've got to go."

"Is it serious?"

"I'll say it is. Why, there are three doctors there already."

Then there was the Polish tennis player who said she'd give her right arm to be ambidextrous.

Q: What religion did Renée Richards practice before his sex-change operation?
A: He was a he, then.

As great a change as Renée underwent, there's no greater contrast in tennis than John McEnroe, who proves that a rich athlete can still be a poor sport.

Q: What's the call when you serve an egg into the net?
A: Omelet.

The young tennis player was courting a young lady.

"Look," he said, "I'm not rich like Ivan Lendl—I don't have a mansion and a chauffeur, or multimillion-dollar endorsement deals. But I love you deeply."

"I love you too," said the woman, "but tell me more about Ivan Lendl."

After winning the U.S. Open, the tennis star got a call from his lawyer.

"I've got good news and bad news," said the attorney. "We nailed down that $5-million endorsement deal . . . but your wife has left you."

"I see," said the athlete. "What's the bad news?"

Q: What do you call a woman tennis player who comes in out of the rain?

A: Dry Martina.

The Polish doubles team served its first ball into the net.

"Don't worry," the server said to his partner, "I always do that. But my second serve never misses."

"Idiot!" screamed the other. "Why don't you just serve your second shot first?"

Then there was a builder who came up with prefab tennis courts. His net profit was astonishing.

Q: What's the difference between a bad shot and an exhausted kangaroo?

A: None. They're both out of bounds.

Q: What did the State Department tell Martina when she wanted to defect?

A: "Sorry, we don't cache Czechs here."

Q: What do you call a gathering of club netmen?

A: A pros anthology.

Q: What's the worst thing about tennis jokes?
A: They're still allowed to pick up a racket.

Q: Who is John McEnroe's greatest fan?
A: His wife's husband.

The truth is, McEnroe never acts irresponsibly on the court. With him, it's the real thing.

To err is human. To blame it on someone else is doubles.

MORE BIG LAUGHS